AUTHOR'S NOTE:

This book is not a step-by-step tutorial on how to use publishing or art programs or how to artistically design a book. Plenty of books have already done that. Rather this is a guide to understanding the basic elements that go into a professional book layout.

Other titles by
Danielle Ackley-McPhail

THE ETERNAL CYCLE SERIES
Yesterday's Dreams
Tomorrow's Memories
Today's Promise

THE ETERNAL WANDERINGS SERIES
Eternal Wanderings

THE BAD-ASS FAERIE TALE SERIES
The Halfling's Court
The Redcap's Queen
The High King's Fool
(forthcoming)

Baba Ali and the Clockwork Djinn
(with Day Al-Mohamed)

The Literary Handyman

The Ginger KICK! Cookbook

SHORT FICTION
A Legacy of Stars
Transcendence
Consigned to the Sea
Flash in the Can
The Die Is Cast
(with Mike McPhail)

The Literary Handyman
Build-a-Book Workshop

Danielle Ackley-McPhail

Pennsville, NJ

PUBLISHED BY
Paper Phoenix Press
A division of eSpec Books
PO Box 242
Pennsville, NJ 08070
www.especbooks.com

Copyright © 2020 Danielle Ackley-McPhail

ISBN: 978-1-949691-19-1
ISBN (ebook): 978-1-949691-18-4

All rights reserved. No part of the contents of this book may be reproduced or transmitted in any form or by any means without the written permission of the publisher.

Interior Design: Danielle McPhail
www.sidhenadaire.com

Literary Handyman Icon: Bryan Prindiville
Cover Art: Greg Schauer
Cover Design: Mike McPhail

Copyediting: Greg Schauer

Dedicated to you,
the brave soul forging your own path
in the publishing world.

Contents

From the Author 1
Preface: The Basics 3

Part One - The Cover

Cover Lexicon 9
Chapter 1 - Putting a Pretty Face on It 13
Chapter 2 - The Fine Details of Composition 21
Chapter 3 - No Junk in the Trunk 25
Chapter 4 - Putting it All Together 33
Cover Checklist 35

Part Two - The Text Block

Text Lexicon 39
Chapter 5 - The Nuts and Bolts 43
Chapter 6 - Typesetting Pitfalls 53
Chapter 7 - Standard Amenities 59
Text Checklist 67

Part Three - Bonus Content

Chapter 8 - But Wait, There's More 73
Afterword 81
Appendix: Avoiding Some Mistakes I've Made 83

About the Author 87
Glossary 89
Construction Crew 96
Index 97

From the Author...

The publishing industry has come through a lot of changes in the last ten or twenty years. So many changes that you could almost say it has returned to its beginnings. You see, when Guttenberg developed his marvelous press and books for the masses became a thing, pretty much every book was self-published. There was no other way. The publishing industry as we recognize it did not take hold until about the 19th century, with vanity presses quick to follow.

Little wonder a stigma developed in the 20th century against self-published works. Most authors had little understanding of how to construct a well-built book, or how to recognize the signs of one poorly done. Vanity presses—a self-published author's only option in the age of sheet-fed or offset printing—are all about quantity over quality. They don't care what your book looks like or if it's any good. They want to produce as many titles as possible as quickly as possible, charging the authors for every step of the process. I say *are* because they've never gone away, they've just changed their tactics and terminology. Be wary of any publisher using the term subsidy press or one who *guarantees* they will get your book into bookstores.

Predatory presses are no longer the only option for authors going the non-traditional route. A lot has changed since those days.

Welcome to the digital age. The 21st century. The DIY era, the era of doing it yourself.

Sadly, many authors still have little understanding of how to construct a well-built book.

Don't be one of them.

We have the knowledge, and the tools are out there. You just need to do a little homework. That's where I come in. I have worked in publishing for nearly thirty years. In that time I have worked at virtually every task there is in the industry. I have also typeset nearly two hundred books at the time I am writing this. This book is my effort to provide you with a blueprint to better design a book. As such, you won't find a lot of actual illustrations as the print book itself employs the elements I describe to you.

Primarily, it is written with fiction books in mind, but I have addressed many design aspects specific to nonfiction as well, so this should be of basic use no matter what you intend to publish.

I hope you enjoy, but most of all, I hope you find this useful!

Danielle Ackley-McPhail
The Literary Handyman*

---

*Because "Handywoman" just doesn't have the same ring.

Preface – The Basics

For simplicity's sake I am going to assume that if you are reading this book you intend—or at least hope—to do the work yourself. If I'm wrong...well, it won't be the first time. Either way, you should still come away knowing how to tell if the job is well done, whether you're doing the work yourself or paying to have it done.

The following are things you may need if you are going to self-publish, start your own press, or freelance as a designer. Not all of them will apply, depending on which aspects you decide to undertake yourself:

- An art program, such as Adobe Photoshop, Corel Photopaint, or a similar program - this is what you will use to create your cover. It allows you to layer text over images and apply special effects features to make your cover pop. It should be able to save or export a file as a PDF, JPEG, or a TIFF, the standard formats you will need. These programs can be expensive and many of them have transitioned to a subscription model. I use Affinity, a program that simulates and in some cases vastly improves on features similar to what you will find in Adobe Photoshop, but for a one-time nominal fee.

- 3D modeling software, such as Daz3d or Poser (optional) - this is so you can pose and light characters for cover art, then take that file into an art program and apply filters and finishing touches to create a final image. Daz is a free program, but it costs to buy the models and accessories you will use in the program. Poser is a program you have to purchase, but it comes with at least a basic library of models.

- Desktop publishing software, such as QuarkXpress or Adobe InDesign – this is to create the interior of the book itself. Programs such as these are a costly investment but are worth it in the long run if you plan to publish books on an ongoing basis. Any word processing program can also be used to generate a book design, but not always with same ease or end result as a program with specialized tools.

- A PDF program, such as Adobe Acrobat or FoxIt – this will let you convert a file to a PDF or allow you to modify a PDF file created by another program. You might need this to process your production files or to create a PDF ebook.

- An ebook conversion program, such as Calibre – newer versions of desktop publishing software can generate an ebook file but can be more complicated to use. Free programs like Calibre convert and manage ebook files from an RTF file and are designed to be easy to use.

- An account with a self-publishing platform, such as Kindle Direct Publishing or Ingram Spark – Once you create your book, you need a way to produce and distribute it. There are quite a few options for this. The two listed are the most commonly used. All of them have pros and cons. Be sure to consider the pros and the cons before you chose one to print with.

- An account with Bowker – This firm manages and supplies ISBNs (International Standard Book Number). Each version of you book is required to have its own unique ISBN. They can be expensive if purchased individually, but do go down in cost when you buy in bulk. Bowker will also offer you other services, such as creating bar codes. These are not needed as places like KDP and Ingram supply you with a bar code when you request a cover template. (More on that later.) Note, many publishing services will provide you with an ISBN for a nominal fee when you use their service, but it is an ISBN they own so they show up as the publisher of your book.

I mention all of this now because they will come up later. Forgive me if some of the information ends up repeated.

Now let's get started!

Part One – The Cover

Cover Lexicon

Rather than have you flip back and forth from where you are reading to the back of the book, at the front of each section you will find a list of terms relevant to that chapter. Not everything will be there, just industry terms that relate to the subject that I may not explain as fully in the chapter itself. A full glossary will also be included at the back.

Bar Code – A graphic representation of the ISBN (see below). It is made up of bars of varying widths that represent the individual numbers that make up the ISBN. It is traditionally printed on the back cover.

Bleed – This is extra space that you add to your cover design where the image or background color extends past the boundary of your final trim size. The bleed is there to provide a safety zone when the cover is trimmed down to size by the printer. This ensures that you do not end up with a white border along the edge of your cover if the trim is a little off.

Blurb – The text that appears on the back cover (or jacket flaps, in the case of a hardcover) that describes the book, enticing the reader to want to know more. Also called Cover Copy, Cover Blurb, Book Blurb, or Jacket Copy.

CMYK – This is a color profile, or mode, that stands for Cyan, Magenta, Yellow, and Black. That means that every color on your cover is made up of different values of some combination of those four colors.

Cover Template – A file provided by the printer showing the exact dimension of your book cover, including guidelines indicating where the cover will be folded and trimmed. Templates also include your basic book data, the bar code matching your ISBN, and markings indicating the minimum safe zones for where you can place your text and important elements of your artwork. Templates are provided electronically as PDFs or InDesign files.

DPI – Stands for Dots Per Inch. The clarity of all images is measured in DPI. The more dots per inch, the clearer an image is. The less dots per inch, the more jaggy an image is. The higher the DPI, the bigger the file will be.

ISBN – International Standard Book Number. A unique identifier assigned by the publisher. Each version of a book requires its own ISBN, which is tied to basic data about the book, such as but not limited to publisher, title, author, format, page count, and price. The ISBN is used by booksellers and librarians to order your book and manage their inventory. All ISBNs are purchased via a service called Bowker. If you purchase from Bowker, the ISBN will show you as the publisher. ISBNs are expensive purchased individually through this service, but the price goes down when you buy in bulk. Standard options are one, ten, and one-hundred ISBNs, with the cost per number going down the more you order at once. If you obtain an ISBN through a publishing service, such as Kindle Direct or Ingram Spark, they are less expensive, or even free, but those numbers indicate that the company you received them from is the publisher of that book, which will also imply to those in the industry that it is self-published, whether it is or not.

Logo – A graphic element representing your brand or imprint. The icon or design should be unique to you. Keep it simple so that it can be scaled up or down as needed and still be legible. It should also be distinct so that it can be readily identified as representing your company. You will want both a black-and-white version, for use in the interior, and a color version, for use on the cover. You will also want to use this logo for advertising purposes.

POD – Print on Demand. This is a digital printing method that allows you to print as few or as many copies as you need. Rather than a printing press, this method makes use of a more advanced copier-type printer where a book prints on standard paper sheets, which are trimmed down to the desired size.

Price-Specific Bar Code – A graphic representation of the ISBN. It is made up of bars of varying widths that represent the individual numbers that make up the ISBN. It also includes additional bars that represent the retail price you have set. You can find free software online that will generate any type of bar code you need. Your printer should also be provided one by your printer if you request a cover template file. There is no need to purchase a bar code, it is an unnecessary expense.

RGB – A color profile, or mode, that stands for Red, Green, and Blue. That means that all the colors on your cover are made up of different values of some combination of these three colors.

Stock Art – Photographs, illustrations, or works of art that have been posted by an artist on a Stock Art website where individuals can purchase a non-exclusive license to use the art for use as interior illustrations or cover art. The cost of the license depends on which rights you wish to purchase and the cost will differ from site to site. There are subscriptions you can sign up for that reduce the overall cost. It is not unusual for artists to create portfolios on multiple sites and there is no limit to how many individuals may license that image. Once you secure the rights to use an image you are able to modify it or combine it with other art to suit your needs but must credit the original artist or artists on the copyright page of your book.

Text Treatment – The words that appear on your cover and any special effects you may employ to embellish them via an art program or internet site.

Trim Size – The final dimensions of your printed book. A standard trim size for a Trade Paperback is six inches by nine inches (or 6 x 9). These dimensions are set, though the actual measurements of the book might vary slightly depending on how precisely the book is trimmed on the production line. The spine width of your book is determined by the weight of your paper and the number of pages in the finished book.

Chapter 1
Putting a Pretty Face on It

It's all well and good to say "don't judge a book by its cover" but you know we all do it, even you (come on, admit it!). That's what it's there for! That is its job! To lure you in and convince you that you might like what's inside. The never-ending question is: Will you be bitterly disappointed, pleasantly surprised, or get what you expect? It's a different story every time, isn't it? No pun intended. Really.

A cover is the first step on a reader's journey. It is their invitation to explore a new world. To this end, it is meant to lure in potential readers. Your cover is your bait. A good cover design will make the reader want to know more. Intrigue them, make them curious. Make them pick up the book. How do you achieve that? How do you stand out — in a good way — from the thousands of books that come out every month? Heck…every day!

I'm going to say this a lot…by doing your homework!

With the sheer volume of books being published each year you have plenty of clear examples of what or what not to do. Just go to your library or your local bookstore or anywhere there is a variety of physical books and browse through the shelves in your chosen genre section. Take a close look. See what draws your eye, what looks good and what doesn't. Does one cover appear more professional compared to another? Learn to recognize what a pretty face is in the publishing world. Books have their own version of symmetry and style. It's constantly changing, but there are certain key points that will always remain the same. I'm going to go through the basic elements of a front cover for you here, just keep in mind that stylistically trends change so it is always a good idea to get a feel for the current market any time you're about to start a project.

For most books there are three basic elements to the front cover: the title, the author's name, and the art. Other things that might appear are a subtitle, series name, a review blurb, or an award the author or book has won…of course, we might be getting ahead of ourselves here. Let's get through your first book.

How to Pick Art

Cover art is often the first thing that gives away a self-published or small-press book. This applies to both the image and the design. We're going to address the art first.

Your challenge is to stay within your budget—whatever that is—without looking like you had one. It doesn't do you any good to save money on art if what you have isn't going to sell books to anyone except friends and family and a few kind-hearted souls who don't want to hurt your feelings.

There are several different ways you can approach cover art:

Stylistic. You can try to capture a style or feel representative of the content, such as making a printed book appear like embossed leather for a steampunk or historic esthetic, or using a tooled metal look for a science fiction book. This avoids the need for actual art and can be accomplished digitally in an art program or by using stock art backgrounds or texture effects. (*Illus. 1.*)

Iconic. If there is a significant symbol (such as a squad icon, heraldry symbol, or tribal marking) in the book, try recreating the image by traditional or digital means, then using an art program to enhance the symbol with etching, embossing, or glow features. This has the added benefits of branding the book with something unique to the story without trying to capture a scene, and saving you money. Just be sure that the finished product looks polished and professional. (*Illus. 2.*)

Danielle Ackley-McPhail 15

Illustration 1 - Stylistic cover.

Using Photoshop effects and a layered file, this cover mimics the look of an embossed leather cover embellished with gold foil in an effort to capture the feel of a 19th century faerie tale book.

For the same reason, the design choice was made to leave the editors names off the cover.

Illustration 2 - Iconic cover.

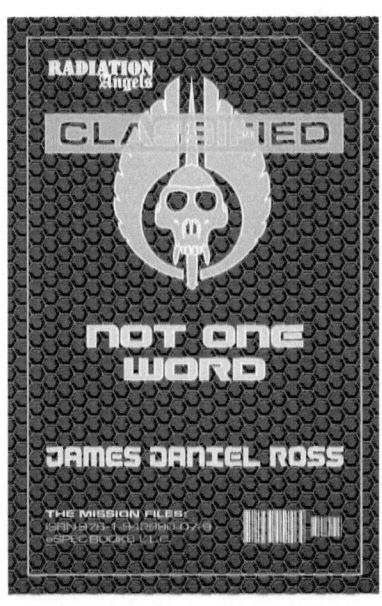

Through texture and design, this cover gives a futuristic military feel and makes use of an established 'squad' icon relevant to the book to brand this and other titles in the series.

In addition, by maintaining this design, then adapting the icon for each project, each title is distinct while still identifiably part of the series.

Illustration 3 - Key Elements cover.

While not representative of a particular scene that takes place in the book, this cover draws on key elements of the story to capture the essential themes of music and magic and the unknown.

Illustration 4 - Montage cover.

For this short story collection, an artist was hired to create a rendition of the author, plus one element from each story in the book, to give an overall feel of the content, without focusing on any individual story.

Key elements. You (or an artist of your choosing) can either create a piece of art representing a scene, or compose a scene that captures the feel of the story without actually depicting something that happened in the book. This can be done through traditional art mediums, digitally in an art program, using a 3D posing program like Daz3d or Poser, or a combination of all three. (*Illus. 3.*)

Montage. That is where you take a few individual images that have relevance to the book and arrange them in an artistic manner. Think of it as a mini story-board you're using to sell the book. (*Illus. 4.*)

In the end, however you approach the cover it should make sense, be clear, clean, engaging, and capture the essence of your book. Above all, it should be eye-catching.

Where to Get Art

Let's face it, most of us don't have any kind of budget for art, let alone a graphics department dedicated to making our books look pretty. You have three options:

Do it yourself. Not a bad option if you have some artistic talent. Super-bad idea if your efforts look like your five-year-old niece was finger-painting. Always consider your skill level before opting to create the cover art yourself. Good for you isn't good *enough*. Bad cover art isn't going to inspire confidence in potential readers. You have to balance the need to save money against the likelihood of selling books.

Pay someone else to do it. If you have a budget, this is always a possibility, particularly if you know a decent artist that will give you a break, or someone with skill trying to build their portfolio. Everyone deserves to be paid for their efforts, but often artists just starting out set crazy-reasonable rates just to get the experience and art credit. This doesn't mean you shouldn't pay them, but it does mean you might be able to afford them. If you find an artist with graphic design training you could negotiate a finished cover, text and all, at a reasonable rate.

If you are hiring an artist, make sure the specifics of the project are spelled out in the contract, including what rights you are purchasing, the details of what you are looking for, what you are allowed to do with the art, and what is and is not included in the artist's fee. Also make sure to request several concept sketches to choose from, to make sure both you and the artist are working toward the same vision. If you are not happy with the results and will not be using the artist's work you can always pay a kill fee (generally half of the agreed-upon price) and look for a new artist.

If you attend fan conventions in your genre, the art show or Artist Alley is a great place to make connections when you are looking for artwork.

Stock art. Don't know any artists? There are so many sites out there that license art and the rates can be quite reasonable. Shutterstock, Adobe, and Fotolia are just a few that I have used. The quality can vary greatly, but if you are patient you can find what you need. Shop around, look for the best deal. Often you can get a subscription, a set number of downloads for low, fixed price. The site I use gives me five images for $50 on a revolving subscription (I use them up, and they charge me $50 for the next batch.)

Is there a lot of dreck out there? Heck yeah! Does it take time and effort to find something that is both good and applicable? You bet! Is it worth it? In a heartbeat! I can't tell you how many book covers we have created with stock art. Sometimes without needing to alter anything. It could take a few hours of searching to find a worthwhile image, but there isn't a project we have done where we couldn't find something that worked as-is or with just the right application of filters. We have even composited several images to achieve the right look for a hard-to-match title. Searches on the stock art platform turn up a lot of image that are low quality or don't apply, but if you look long enough you can find something. I have even found traditional art and images that have already been put through filters to simulate an art feel. And new content is being uploaded all the time.

Learn from Others' Mistakes

While I am sure all presses have a gallery of shame when it comes to bad cover designs, there are some practices that seem endemic of small press. Avoid doing the following if you want to raise the bar in small press or independent publishing cover design:

Using a 3D posing image as final art. 3D modeling software is meant to create the foundation for finished art, not be used as the end product. This goes hand in hand with using a bad 3D posing image as art. If you are going to use this tool, use it right. Make the poses natural, not too stiff, rigid, or awkward, and always take the image into an art program and use filters and effects to finish that image and give it life. Raw 3D posing images inherently look fake, flat, and untextured. A lot of small presses and self-published authors make this mistake. Don't be one of them. Avoiding just this one mistake will elevate you above most of the independent books out there.

Using unaltered photographs. Most personal photographs just don't have a finished feel. If you are going this route, you really want to clean up the image and enhance it with effects to enhance the final product, perhaps even compositing the image with other photographs or digital elements to create a more cohesive and relevant feel for the cover, otherwise it can come across like you did the project on your home computer. No matter how accurate that may be, you don't want it to appear that way.

Using stock art that has been used as cover art by others. This is a bit harder to avoid, but try. If you are considering using a stock image search the image in your web browser to see if any other covers come up. You can do this by dragging the image file up to the search field. Another approach to avoid this issue is to composite the image with other stock art to create something new or crop the original image so that you are onlyusing a piece of it.

Getting the details wrong. If you are basing your cover art on characters, details, or events in your book, make sure they match. Little things like hair and eye color or skin tone matter. Readers assume the character on the front of the book matches the one inside. They get annoyed when they don't match up. Details like this are very easily altered in most art programs so there really is no reason not to get it right. Remember, yes, it has to look good, but it also has to make sense!

Lack of contrast. All the elements of a cover should work together, if the art image and/or the text doesn't have enough contrast you end up with a 'muddy' or flat cover. That's where it is hard to figure out what is going on or difficult to read the text because it is fighting or blending in with a portion of the image behind it.

Using confusing art. This is usually caused by two possible things. First, using a cover image that doesn't visually make sense or can't readily be identified for what it is. Second, art with a style, tone, or composition that conflicts with the content or genre of the book so that the potential reader doesn't know what to make of it. When they are left confused the book is generally left on the shelf. Or, if it isn't, you could lose their future business if the cover gave them one expectation and the book delivers another.

Chapter 2
The Fine Details of Composition

Once you have your art, it is time to consider your design. By this, I mean what is going on your cover and where. As I mentioned earlier, the text treatment will be the title and the author's name. Where those appear on the book depends on the composition of the art. You want the text to flow harmoniously with the artwork, rather than fighting against it. Your best bet — if you are doing the design yourself — is to open the image in your art program and play with it (always on a copy, never on the master file.)

Look first for natural negative space, the open areas around the image itself. This is always the first option when placing text. One, you aren't covering anything up, and two you are filling an empty space in the art in a way that allows the text to work with the image. Just don't fill up too much space. You don't want your cover to look cluttered. It's all about balance.

Another option is to place the text over an unimportant part of the image, one where it's not going to cover up too much of the central detail. An example would be across the top, where there is sky or trees or whatever makes up your background, or across the bottom where there is floor or some other element of the image people don't really need to see.

A third option is to have the text interact with the image in some way. This is where your art program comes in handy. By creating layers, you can duplicate parts of the image to overlap the text or you can use the effects tools to give the text a similar treatment to an aspect of the art. With tricks like this you integrate the text so that it becomes one with the image.

Design is as much a creative process as a technical one, you don't have to limit yourself. As long as the final design works to create a cohesive professional-looking cover with good flow, there are no real rules, just standard conventions. This is where you want to look at examples of what other people have done. Not just to get ideas, but to also know what to avoid.

Readability

Is your text easy to read? Back in the day when typesetting meant literally setting metal blocks of type, the guideline for designing a title treatment was, can you read it from six feet away? Basically, from across a bookstore aisle, would you know what book you are looking at? While bookstores aren't as much of a concern these days, the premise still applies, only we aren't concerned about six feet away. Now the question is can you still read the title clearly in a thumbnail? Because face it, for many people, buying books these days is done from a computer screen… or heck, from their phone. Thumbnails are generally one inch by one and a half inches in dimension or smaller. A good cover will be recognizable at that size, if not legible.

How do you achieve that? First you pick a font that is clean and easy to read. One without superfine detail that will disappear against the background or when reduced. A font that will complement the content of your book and pair well with the artwork. Most computers come with a wide range of fonts already installed, but if you are downloading one online make sure that it is either free for commercial use or that you are paying for a license that allows for commercial use. Once you've chosen your font you can play with the many features in an art program to accent the title, such as embossing, drop shadow, glow, etc. Sometimes, depending on what art is in the background, even the cleanest font will need embellishing to stand out. A simple outline can make the words more crisp and readable, or you might need to create a frame because the background image is too busy.

Another aspect of readability is contrast. Do the elements on the cover stand out individually? You don't want the title or author's name to get lost against a busy background, but you also don't want them to distract from the art image. Just remember, the elements of the cover should work together, not compete.

The final consideration is flow. Is there a natural path that your eye travels when looking at the cover? Do the elements focus you toward a specific point, or do they individually compete for your attention? Every cover should have a focal point. That single element that grabs the eye and makes the reader want to look closer. All aspects of your design should work together toward that one end.

The Spine

Much like the human backbone, the spine of the book is what holds everything together and makes it work. If you are producing electronic books only, skip this section. It is not relevant to you.

If you are producing print books, the spine is where the book is bound together. Originally, books were literally bound… or sewn together. Now they are glued to keep all the pages in place. As far as cover design is concerned, a basic spine includes only three things: the title, the author's full or last name (depending on available space), and the publisher's imprint (generally in the form of an icon). In the case of thick mass-market paperbacks, the publisher might include a thumbnail of the cover art. One other optional element, if space allows and it is applicable, would be to include a volume number if the book is part of a series. If the title is particularly long you might consider leaving off the author's first name on the spine, rather than cram things too close together.

Readability is the most important aspect here. The spine is what most people will see when the book is on a bookshelf. You want to make sure the text is clear, easy to read, and doesn't come too close to the edge of the spine, otherwise the words could partially fold over to the front or back of the book if the binder is not precise when they place and trim the cover. Sadly, this is more common with print-on-demand printing.

Chapter 3
No Junk in the Trunk

If step one in a reader's journey is picking up the book, step two is turning it over. The front cover is the bait. The back cover is the hook. This is the first place the potential reader goes for more information. Not just how much the book costs or who publishes it, but to find out what the book is about.

That text on the back is called a cover blurb or jacket copy. It is important to understand what job that text is supposed to do. This is not a full description of the book. You are not telling the reader what happens. This is your teaser, a playful little dance to entice them, to make them want to know more. To follow the fishing metaphor, the cover blurb is your lure. Needless to say, cover blurbs aren't easy to write. How much do you tell? How much do you imply? Where do you stop? There is a fine art to writing cover copy. It's not a book report. It's more like a movie trailer.

You want to introduce the main character, their objective, and the threat to that goal, but in a jazzy way that sounds exciting without giving any deeper details. I generally start with a banner for visual interest and to break up the copy so it isn't just a solid block, then I feed out some teasers with a little flare, using more lyrical language rather than straight prose, and I finish with a question. In truth, if I have done my job right, all the reader has is questions…and a desire to know more! Here, let me give you an example:

Mortal. Immortal. Musician. Mage.

On a journey from the boroughs of New York to the heart of Tir na nÓg, from innocence to the deepest darkest crevices of her soul, Kara O'Keefe found power and strength in the discovery of self. But with that peace came a hard truth. As a bridge connecting many worlds, none of them held a place for her.

She must find her own way, forge her own path.

To honor a vow to Granddame Rose, a matriarch of the Kalderaš Clan, Kara joins the Romani caravan, only to find herself even more of an outsider than before. While she strives for acceptance, and to honor her vow, little does she know she has once more become a lure to an ancient and deadly enemy, drawing danger into the midst of her unsuspecting hosts.

Once savior of the world, Kara must now save herself and the innocents around her.

She has come into her legacy, but where will destiny take her?

(Back cover text for *Eternal Wanderings* by Danielle Ackley-McPhail, Paper Phoenix Press)

Now, this might not suit your style, or the tone of your writing, but the basic construction would work for any book. Banner, brief introduction, setup, conflict, question. Again, the end goal is to leave them wanting more. If the front cover is meant to make them pick up the book, the back is meant to make them open it. To do that you can't give too much away. You want brief and punchy. I usually aim for between 100 and 150 words, give or take.

There are two reasons for this, one, you don't want to give too much away; and two, you want to leave room for everything else that needs to go back there without things being too cluttered. So…shall we get into the technical bits?

Back Cover Design Elements

Please note: I am only touching on basics here because an entire book could be written just about cover design... and I'm sure someone already has. That having been said, there are certain details you want to include on the back cover:

Artwork. (Optional.) The back cover can be a solid color, an artistic treatment, or art that wraps around from or mirrors the front cover. This is the designer's choice. If there is artwork behind the text, make sure it is subtle and does not make the text difficult to read, or use something like a screen or shadow technique between the text and the art to make the text stand out.

A Banner. (Optional.) A tag line or banner at the top can catch the eye and draw the reader in. It can also help frame the text and give it visual interest and style.

The Cover Blurb. We've already talked about this, basically it is your sales pitch. The text should be clean, easy to read, and not compete with the background. Don't make the font too small or too large. It can be justified text or centered or freeform to run around a graphic element on the back. It doesn't really matter as long as the design is clear and makes sense, with the text and any graphic elements working together to create an appropriate feel.

Author Biog. (Optional) If you have too much blank space on the back of your book, you could put a brief author bio after the cover blurb. If you do, make it concise and professional, not your full bio, but the highlights. Awards, bestsellers, things that may impress a potential reader. That means you don't include that your book was a Reader Choice selection on an obscure web site, but you do include that it was a Recommended Read in an industry magazine that carries weight in your chosen genre. Same goes for awards. If you won a local writing contest...or one in school, I wouldn't mention that, but if you won a national or international award, by all means! Don't let the bio take over the back cover, though. These days most publishers put them in the backmatter of the book, that is where your extended biography should go.

Your Imprint. Whether you are setting up your own press or just self-publishing your work, you need an imprint. This is the brand you will publish work under. All traditional publishers have what are called imprints, that is a name and a logo representing that company or brand. In fact, larger publishers have multiple imprints, each one known for a different type or genre of book, so potential readers know they can look for that imprint and find the kind of thing they like to read. Most potential readers will look for this information to see if the publisher is one they recognize and perhaps already trust. The absence of an imprint is a red flag that a book is less than "professional". This could lead some to make unfounded assumptions about the quality of your book.

ISBN and Bar Code. All books sold commercially are required to have an ISBN (International Standard Book Number), a unique identifier that allows bookstores and libraries to quickly access information about your book, including author, title, and publisher. This is the number they need to order the book. The bar code is a graphic representation of that number that can be scanned with the proper equipment and read by a computer. It appears on the back of your book, generally in the lower right-hand corner or the bottom middle of the cover. Commercial retailers have very specific requirements. For them to order the book, the bar code must be what is called 'price-specific'. That means that in addition to your author, title, and publisher information, the bar code has an extra portion that includes the price. As most places use scanners to scan the bar code for both sales and inventory purposes they generally will not order books that do not have price-specific bar codes because they cannot easily input it in their system or track their sales.

Non-Distribution SKU – a Stock Keeping Unit is a number similar to an ISBN that is used to track information for a book that will not be distributed commercially. In other words, the number is for internal purposes and will not be used by an outside party to look up or order your book. Most online printers will generate one of these numbers for you if you do not provide an ISBN but only you will be able to order stock. You would use this to produce special stock you intend to sell directly.

Price. Even though, with hope, you have included a price-specific bar code, it is a good idea to also include the actual price on the cover of your book for the potential reader who may not know how to identify the price in the bar code.

Genre. (Optional) Most potential readers should be able to tell genre based on your cover art and back cover copy, but some publishers like to include a genre designation on the back cover. In most cases genre is more for bookstores and libraries anyway, so they know where to shelve the book, but it is nice to clarify for the reader, just in case they are getting a different impression from the cover.

Website. (Optional) Is it required? No. Is it a good idea? It can be. It depends on how professional your site is and how serious you are about publishing. It could be specific to the book/series, you as an author, or you as a publisher. If you are going to include it on the cover of the book it should be a dedicated custom domain, not a social media site or page on an unrelated site. Those would appear unprofessional. You also want to ensure that you are only providing links to sites that have a professional appearance, without errors, missing images, or broken links.

Artist credit. (Optional.) This doesn't have to go on the back cover, as long as it appears on the copyright page, but it is a nice gesture to the artist and fosters good will.

Award Citation. If your book has been a finalist or winner of a reputable award that is definitely information you want to include on your cover. Same thing goes for bestseller status, but only for something big. If you make a bestseller list in a mainstream or applicable industry publication (such as *The New York Times*, *USA Today*, or *Locus Magazine*, for example) that you want to include. If you made your hometown's bestseller list, best to leave it off. It's not going to win you any brownie points with potential readers or industry professionals.

Review Blurbs. (Optional.) Tread carefully here. You don't want to clutter your book, but if you receive a favorable review from a respected source like an A-list author or an industry magazine like *Publishers Weekly* or an applicable genre magazine like *Analog*, that is something you want to include. Be wary, though. There are some professional review sites that require payment for a review. That may or may not be in your best interest. I always recommend pursuing free review options first as the pay sites can be quite hefty and may not give you a positive return on your investment.

Now that you know what to include, let's talk about how it should appear. (*Illus. 5.*) In the end, you want to keep it clean and simple, including details that will increase your chances of selling that book, without cramming on so much that that the back looks cluttered. Always aim for a professional look.

Illustration 5 - cover design. This example labels the basic elements of the front, spine, and back cover and gives you some idea of how they would be arranged. To make room for elements such as award citations or review blurbs, the existing copy would be resized or truncated.

A. Cover Blurb
B. Banner
C. Spine Title
D. Front Title
E. Price
F. Website
G. Art Credits
H. Imprint/Logo
I. Genre
J. Price-Specific Bar Code
K. Spine Logo
L. Spine Author Name
M. Front Author Name
N. Art

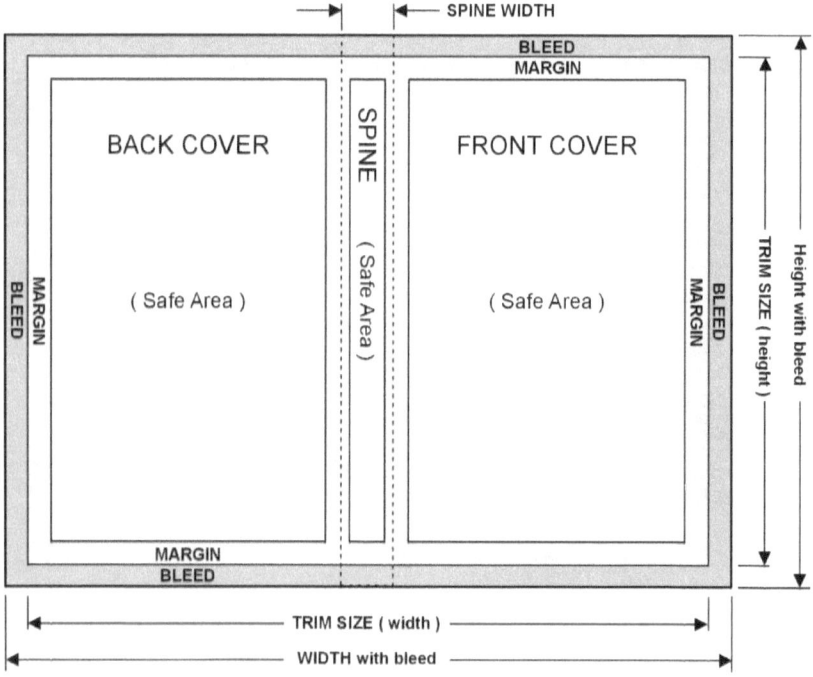

Illustration 6 - cover template. This is a generic example of the template a printer may provide. It is created to the specific dimensions of your book based on the page count and the paper you selected when you set up your title. Your finished design is layered over top of the template so that when the cover is printed the workers on the binding line know where to cut and fold the cover so it fits on the finished book.

Chapter 4
Putting it All Together

When you are preparing your files for production, standard practice is to request a cover template from the printer you are working with. (*Illus. 6.*) They generate this based on the page count, trim size, and weight of the paper you have selected for your project. This gives them the final dimensions of the printed book.

The template they provide uses those dimensions to give you a diagram of where the different elements of your cover need to be placed. There are crop marks showing you where the final edge—or the trim—of your cover is, where the fold points for the spine are, and where your bleed is (all industry-specific terms I use appear in the lexicon at the beginning of each section, as well as in the glossary at the end of the book). It shows you the safe areas where all of your text and critical image elements need to fall within. That having been said, that does not mean you should run your text right up to that line. If you do, your book will definitely look unprofessional. Always leave a quarter- to a half-inch margin all around the text on the front and back covers. Also on the template is the ISBN/Bar code for your book. You can reposition this by saving just the bar code and importing it as a separate layer on your final cover file. Do this stage last as the bar code needs to be unaltered to work. Most places will want you to save the cover file as a PDF.

If you need ideas on how a book cover should be designed, look at a variety of books in your genre. That truly is the best way to get an idea of what is done short of taking an actual design class. Use your critical eye. Look at a wide selection of covers and take note of things like text treatment, art, and placement of the individual elements. Get an idea of what works and what doesn't. The best way to do that is with actual examples of things that have already been published. Don't look just at one publisher, seek out different imprints. Look for names you don't recognize so you are sure to get a wide range of examples that run the gambit from successful to unsuccessful.

Preparing Final Files

First and foremost, whatever print service you are using, they should have guidelines that tell you how they want to receive the final files to produce your book. Find those guidelines and read them. It will make the process that much smoother.

These guidelines will specify everything from file format to DPI to minimum margins, etc. Generally, they want you to provide the print cover files in PDF or TIFF format, in CMYK mode, 300 DPI. For ebooks they request JPEG format, in RGB mode.

If you aren't sure what you are supposed to do, read the guidelines and then call tech support to make sure you are doing it correctly.

Cover Checklist

Front Cover

- Is the text treatment easy to read?
- Is the text too close to the edges of the book?
- Is the artwork engaging?
- Is the artwork applicable to the book?
- Can you identify what the image is?
- Does the text treatment detract from the art or complement it?
- Can you read the physical cover from six feet away?
- Can you read the digital cover as a thumbnail?

Back Cover

- Is the text treatment easy to read?
- Is the text too close to the edges of the book?
- Do you have a hook or noteworthy review blurb?
- Is the back cover copy enough to catch the reader's attention without telling too much?
- Have you included an icon representing your company or brand?
- Have you included a price-specific bar code?

- Have you included the book price?
- Have you included your website?

Spine

- Is the title readable from six feet away?
- Is the author legible?
- Have you included an icon representing your company or brand?

Part Two - The Text Block

Text Lexicon

Acknowledgements – This generally goes at the front of the book, though some publishers choose to put it at the back. It is a list or written section where you acknowledge those who helped make the book possible, helped work on it, or supported you while you wrote it.

Appendixes – This is additional or expanded information presented at the end of the book. It is a way for the author to share research, theories, or back story without interrupting the flow of the story or text when the additional information might not be immediately relevant, just of interest.

Back matter – The extra content located at the back of your book, such as but not limited to the author's biography, Appendixes, Glossary, or Index. Content that is separate from your story or nonfiction, but complements it.

Chapter/Story Title – The identifying text that appears on the first page of your chapter, story, or article, depending on if you are producing a novel, collection/anthology, or nonfiction work.

Contents Page – Also called the Table of Contents. The list of sections that appear in your book, including titles and page numbers. If the book involves contributions by multiple individuals, the author's name would appear following the title of their work. This only includes materials that come after the contents page.

Copyright Page – The page following the title page, including the relevant details and disclaimers required in publishing, such as, but not limited to, the publisher's contact information, the copyright notice, the relevant ISBNs, Library of Congress Control Number, and legal disclaimers, also included are the credits for the cover art, any illustrations, the editor, and the designer(s).

Drop Cap – When the first letter of the first word on a page is larger and inset into the first paragraph by two or more lines. Often the font is different and more ornate than that used for the base text. Take care which font you choose as some have florishes that will obsure the surrounding text. The font should be easy to read and complement the feel of the book.

Facing Pages – These are pages that will be visible side by side when you open the book. In other words, you can see them at the same time without turning the page. You can think of it this way, if you close the book they are facing each other. Well…more than facing, but what happens behind closed covers…

Folio – The technical term for the page number.

Front Matter – The extra content located at the front of a book, such as but not limited to the title page, Table of Contents, dedication, maps, list of characters, list of terms, or pronunciation guides. This material is generally numbered with lowercase roman numerals when there is a page number on the page. A running head or page number is generally only used if the element (such as the contents page) is longer than one page.

Full-Bleed – When a background or image extends all the way to the edge of the printed page. To allow for this and make sure there is no white space where there shouldn't be, the designer extends the background or image a quarter inch past the desired trim size of the book.

Glossary – A list of terms that generally appears in the back matter giving greater detail regarding terms or concepts depicted in the book.

Gutter Margin – The extra space you should add to your text design on the inside edge of the page where the book will eventually be bound. Typically, you would add a quarter of an inch or more depending on the thickness of the book. This extra space allows the book to be bound without the text disappearing into the binding of the book.

Half-Title Page – The same as the title page, but with only the title of the book printed on it, not the author and the publisher. When there is a half-title page, it is generally the first page in the book, followed by a blank page, a list of other titles by the author, or a quote or image the author wishes to start off the book with. Half-title pages are a legacy from offset or sheet-fed printing, where a book's pagination must be in increments of four-, eight-, or sixteen-page signatures. If there are too many blank pages at the end of the book (which looks bad) a half-title page is included in the front matter to adjust the signatures and reduce the number of blank pages in the back. In digital printing a half-title page might be included if there is some design element the author or publisher wants to include on the page facing the title page.

Imprint – The brand under which the book is being produced. Sometimes this is the publisher's name, but sometimes a publisher will create a separate sub-brand to group books by genre or type.

Index – These are used for nonfiction, textbooks, and cookbooks. It is a list of the relevant terms in the book and where they are discussed so that readers can go directly to the passages that may contain the information they are looking for.

Introduction – Some books will have an introduction. In most cases, these are collections or nonfiction books. The introduction may be written by the author, or by a notable individual, such as a professional in the industry or a well-known author.

Layout – 1. How the elements of your book are arranged on the page. 2. The act of arranging the elements of your book, including placement and style.

Logo – A graphic representation of a publisher or imprint.

Margins – The blank space running around the edge of the text block denoting the edge of the page.

Review Blurbs – Occasionally, a book will include advance reviews or reviews of a previous edition. When these are particularly favorable and from a reputable source, publishers will often include these at the beginning of the book on the first page following the front cover.

Running Foot – When the page numbers appear consecutively at the bottom of the printed page.

Running Head – The text and/or page number that appears at the top of the printed page. For novels, it generally contains the title of the book on one page and the author's name on the facing page, both accompanied by the page number. For collections or anthologies, it generally contains the title of the book on one page with the story or article title and author on the facing page, both accompanied by the page number.

Section Break – A decorative element that appears between two separate sections of text, generally in a work of fiction. It can be a font-generated symbol or an actual art graphic that complements the theme of the book.

Style Guides – In many desktop publishing programs—if not all—there are tools where you can define the formatting for different aspects of your book so that when they reoccur all you need to do is select the correct style and the formatting will be implemented. The style guides also allow you to change the style of an element in one place and have it automatically apply to all instances of that style.

Templates – In many desktop publishing programs—if not all—you can create a standard template, or Master, for a type of page in your book that you can drop into place as needed changing the existing layout to the desired layout.

Title Page – This page includes the basic identifying information of a book. In most cases, the title, series, book number (where applicable), the author or editor's name, the imprint and the publisher's location.

Chapter 5
The Nuts and Bolts

You've opened a book some time in your life. I know you have. You can't deny it. If nothing else, I know you have opened *this* book. If you stop to think about it, we all know what a book should look like. The problem is we've seen so many that the fine details of what goes where blend into the background. Unless they are wrong, then they really stand out.

There are some elements of book design that *should* blend into the background. If they don't, they should at least work with the text to create a cohesive feel, not compete with the text for the reader's attention.

Title/Chapter. Depending on what you are publishing, you will have either a Story or Chapter Opening Page. On the first page, the text starts roughly a third to halfway down the page and the story title, chapter title, or chapter number appears somewhere in the white space above it. Where and how it appears in that white space is a design choice. Titles/Chapters are generally in a more stylized font that matches the tone or genre of the content, but should always be clear and easy to read. If possible, I match this font to what was used on the front cover.

Author Name. If the publication includes works by multiple authors, such as an anthology or textbook, the author name will appear beneath the applicable title. The font will generally be smaller and simpler than the title font, but larger than the text font. Again, placement is a design choice.

Text Block. The main text of your book, consisting of words, sentences, and paragraphs. Yeah, I know…duh! But it had to be said. The text should be justified (the lines align straight down both sides of the page), single-spaced, indented, with no extra line space between paragraphs (that is an online convention.)

Some designers make the choice to leave the first paragraph of a story, chapter, or section without an indent to reinforce that it is the beginning or to accommodate a Drop Cap, where the first letter or word of the first paragraph is larger that the rest and drops down into the lines below. This is a stylistic choice and fits industry standards. As long as you do it consistently, it will not be seen as a design error.

If the text block is too solid, with long paragraphs and little white space to break it up, it can be a strain for the reader, leading to eye fatigue. If this occurs, consider looking at your paragraphs to see if they can be broken up into several shorter paragraphs, or, in the case of fiction, if there is an opportunity to interject some dialogue to break things up.

Finally, keep in mind is that the text blocks on facing pages need to align with one another across the bottom of the pages.

Alignment. There are four type alignments in typesetting. Left, Right, Center, and Justified.

- Left and Right are where the indicated edge lines up (or aligns) and the other edge is ragged (the sentences end when there is no room for the next word on the line.)
- Center is where neither edge aligns but the middle of the sentence lines up with the center of the page.
- Justified is when the spacing between the words adjusts so that both edges of the text block align to create a solid rectangle.

The first three alignments are most typically used for design elements like the Title/Chapter, Author, quotes, lines of verse, or section breaks. When it comes to the text block, it should always be justified.

Font. To meet industry standard, text fonts should be a simple, easy-to-read serif font. That is a font with the little extra bumps and points on it, for those not familiar with the term. Serif fonts are more usually used for print books because they are easier to read over long periods. Sans Serif font (those that are just lines without embellishment) can be hard on the eyes after a while. You also don't want to use a fancy font for your text block. Most of them are not very legible in smaller point sizes and you don't want the reader to become frustrated by difficult to read text.

The next concern is the size of the text. Back in the day, when typesetting was literally putting together little metal blocks to form the words, font (or point) sizes were uniform. Most text was printed in 10 point font with a 12 point leading (the leading was actual lead bars placed between the sentences to space them out.) This presented a uniform and consistent page that was easy to read. In the digital age fonts are no longer consistent. 10 point in one font is a completely different size from 10 point in another. Because of this, text that is digitally set can be anywhere from 10 point to 14 point in size. Whatever point size you use, the leading should be two points higher. In the end, it is all about readability.

Some standard fonts used today are Garamond, Bookman Old Style, and Book Antiqua. Font to avoid are Times New Roman (generally used for journalism), Courier and other "typewriter" fonts, overly ornate or script-type fonts like *Brush Script* or *Freestyle Script* that will distract from the content or make it difficult to read.

Indent. Formatting styles have transformed over the years. Originally, there was just manuscript format and print format. Then people developed their own formatting style for online viewing and it further confused matters. Sometimes they forget (or never knew) that print formatting is different from either manuscript or digital. Do not use manuscript or digital format for a published book. It will stand out as self-published and unprofessional. A print paragraph is typically indented a quarter of an inch.

Spacing. I have addressed this briefly already, so forgive me if I repeat myself as I go into greater detail. Text in a published book should be single-spaced, generally with a leading (extra padding) two points larger than the font size but can be selectively adjusted if the text block is a little too dense, or you need to adjust how the text lands on the page. To correct a typesetting issue—such as a header separated from its text or facing text blocks not ligning up across the bottom of the pages—you can increase or decrease the spacing by up to a point in either direction without it being too noticeable. Double-spaced lines should not be used in a published book.

The other type of technical spacing is kerning, where you adjust the space between individual letters to achieve a more pleasing visual or to correct for other typesetting issues, such as too much hyphenation, bad breaks, and widows and orphans (don't worry, I'll explain later).

Line spacing is another matter, as in having a blank line between design elements. As already mentioned, paragraphs should not be followed by a line space. Here are the exceptions. If you have a quote or other type of insert that breaks up the text block and changes format, a blank line before and after sets off the element and makes it evident the change in formatting is intentional. Examples would be lyrics, a letter or journal entry, a flashback, tables or other illustrations.

Margins. In publishing, for a trade paperback book, the margin on a text page is half an inch on the top, bottom, and outside edge. The inside edge, where the book will be bound, has a three-quarter inch margin. The extra margin is called a gutter margin and is added so that when the book is bound text and images do not disappear into the crease, where the pages curve. This is called bottling. If you make your margins too big, it will appear you are padding the book to make it longer…putting fewer words on a page so that there are more pages. If you don't put enough of a margin, the page will look too dense and your text and images could disappear into the gutter. Both of these instances make your finished product look unprofessional and can lead to an unsatisfactory experience for your reader.

Running Head. This is the information printed at the top of every text page *except* the Title/Chapter Opening Page or blank pages. In a novel, the book title typically appears at the top of the left-hand page and the author's name appears at the top of the right-hand page. In an anthology, collection, or textbook, the book title would be in the same place, and the story or chapter title would be on the facing page, along with the author's name if the book includes multiple authors.

The placement of the running head is below the top margin, about a quarter of an inch above the text block. This information can be centered or appear at the outside edge of the page. You could align it on the inside of the page (where the binding is), but this may prove difficult to read. While you can use a more stylized font, make sure it is legible in a smaller point size. If possible, I usually match this font to the one used on the cover or Title/Chapter Opening Page.

There is some room here for creative design. My best recommendation is to look at other published examples and be guided by what looks good to you. In the end, all elements of the design should work together to create the proper tone and feel for the reader's experience.

For consistency, create templates or style guides in your design program so you are only entering data for each element once.

I generally create two templates for a novel, Chapter Opening Page and Text Page (which is for anything that is not a Chapter Opening.) If there are back matter elements that would have customized running heads, I create templates for those too.

For anthologies, I create a separate Text Page template for each story in the book and any relevant back matter so that I can customize the running heads.

Page Number. These would appear either in the running head, at the outside edge of each page, or in the running foot, centered on the page. If you use a stylized font for the running head, make sure it includes numbers and they are clearly identifiable. If they are not, use a different, simpler font for the page numbers. Most word processing or design and layout programs have a feature that will automatically number your pages if you add the code to the design.

Section Break. In fiction, scene breaks will occasionally happen. As a part of your design, these breaks should be clearly marked in some manner. In many instances, publishers use a simple or decorative graphic element that works with the overall design of the book. This is the method I recommend, otherwise it can be confusing if the reader misses that there has been a break, as can happen if the break occurs at the bottom or top of a page, particularly in the case of an ebook. A graphic element makes it clear there has been a change.

If you chose not to use a graphic element and instead denote section breaks with an extra line space between, I would recommend formatting the first line of the next section in a distinct manner to make it clear it is the start of a new section. Examples would be to have the first line in small capital letters (small caps), italic, or bold, or to use a drop cap on the first letter of the first paragraph of the new section.

Quotes/Lyrics/Poetry/Correspondence. If you are quoting an outside source of one of these types, a line or two is quoted within the text, and three lines or more is offset from the main body of the text, separated from it with a blank line before and after the quote. Often the quote is also indented on both sides to further distinguish it from the body of the text.

- Quotes – These could appear at the beginning of a chapter/story, or within the body of the text. The formatting is stylistic. Some people use italics, others use quotation marks, some use both. Pick a style that suits you (or refer to a style guide), and remain consistent.

- Poetry/Lyrics – When interjected within the text, the formatting for poetry is usually indented and/or centered, in stanzas, with a blank line before the piece, between stanzas, and after the piece.

- Correspondence – This could be any kind of communication: a letter, memo, email, or journal entry. The text is set off from the body of the text with a line space above and below and indented on either side. The font is often in italics or in some other way different from the text body. Some use a script type font, but if you do so, ensure it is simple and easy to read.

Numbered/Bullet Lists.

- The list is set off from the body of the text with a line space above and below and indented on either side.
- The text of the list aligns on the first word of the first line, not the bullet.
- A number, dot, or some other symbol sets off the points of the list.

Footnotes/Endnotes. When you have a note, citation, or reference that applies to a specific point in your text you use a superscript numeral to indicate the text to which the footnote or endnote applies. A footnote would be placed at the bottom of the page as a full-sized number, a period, a space, and then the full citation (if you are referring to an outside source) or the text of your footnote if it is just a note providing additional information. If the same source is referenced throughout the book, the first use of the footnote is a full citation and subsequent footnotes are an abbreviated citation. (What a full or abbreviated citation includes or how it is formated is dependent on the particular style guide you elect to follow, i.e. *Chicago Manual of Style*, etc.)

If you prefer to have the notes appear in a separate section in the back of the book, all of the above still applywith the noted exception of where the note is printed.

Embellishment. (Optional) Many traditional publishers shy away from artistic embellishments in their designs. They are an additional expense that will add to the bottom line, without increasing the monetary value of the end product (ie: you can't charge more for a book just because you've made it pretty.)

However, that having been said, it is done. A graphic embellishment repeated on each title/chapter opening page, done properly, can increase the professional appearance of a book and add to the reader's experience by supporting the tone of the book, when matched properly with the content. Embellishments can be a graphic flourish or icon that comes as a part of a font package or simple line art licensed from a stock art site. It can also be a custom graphic element created by an artist to your specifications based on the content of the book, either line art accent pieces or even page borders (preferably only on the Title/Chapter Opening Page). Some publishers make the design choice to have a different embellishment on each Title/Chapter Opening Page, customized to the text that follows. Your call. If you use an embellishment make sure it is professional, complementary, and well-done. If you use multiple embellishments, make sure they match in style and quality. If not, you are much better off not using them.

Illustrations. (Optional) I have always loved illustrated volumes. To me, they enhance the experience, making it richer. That having been said, I wouldn't sink big money into them. If you include pictures, they should be high resolution, well-executed, with good contrast and line density so that they reproduce well, something that can be a challenge with POD production. If the effort is amateurish, you are better off without them. While illustrations don't add to the value of a book, bad ones can certainly detract from it.

With nonfiction books, things are a little different. Sometimes illustrations exist to clarify, supplement, or demonstrate information being explained in the text. When this is the case, clearly mark all graphic images with a number or letter and include that citation at the relevant text mention. Always cite your source and be sure to secure permission or license to use anything you haven't generated yourself. All images should be clear and in high resolution (300 DPI). If there are multiple illustrations or graphic elements in the book, make them consistent with one another. If you include illustrations of different styles and quality it can make the work look unprofessional.

Graphic images can come in many different forms:

- Photographs – Unless you have taken the photograph yourself, be sure to secure permission or a license to use any photographs included in your work. Also, always cite the source and/or copyright, where applicable.

- Art – Whether an illustration or a graphic of some sort, make sure all lines are sufficiently thick, clean, and crisp to reproduce well and anything not line art has good contrast and clarity.

- Tables – if using tables or charts, be sure to include a key, where applicable, and make sure everything is clearly labeled.

- Timelines/Family Tree – These may be text-based or image-based, but should be consistent throughout.

Summing up

Design is an art, what works for one project may not be appropriate for the next. As long as the end product appears professional when you are done, with all the elements working in concert with one another in a consistent manner, there is no one right way.

The best way to accomplish this is by using the tools in your design program to their fullest potential. Once you establish a format, create templates and style guides locking in those settings, that way when you encounter that element as you work you can use those short cuts to implement the correct design.

Chapter 6
Typesetting Pitfalls

There are a number of design *faux pas* that will instantly give a work away as self-published or small press. Not that the traditional publishers haven't been guilt of them as well, but it is generally less common because they have dedicated staff or freelancers whose job it is to specifically look for such things.

I have already mentioned some of these in the previous chapters, but I am addressing them separately here to go into more detail.

Bad Breaks. This could manifest in a variety of ways, but basically it is when the text cuts to the next page in an unfortunate way. Here are some examples:

- There is not enough room for the section break at the bottom of the page so it migrates to the top of the next page, leaving extra white space at the bottom of the previous page.
- The page ends with a header or section title at the bottom of the page, but the relevant text at the top of the next page.
- The first line of a poem or an insert prints at the bottom of the page and the rest appears on the next page.
- All of the words from a sentence remain on one line, while the punctuation is all alone on the next line.

These are just a few of the ways you can end up with bad breaks, but by no means are they the only ways. You will have to use your judgement and address the issues accordngly. But in the end, any break that is visually unpleasing or awkward should be dealt with.

Bad Hyphenation. Hyphens are a fact of life with justified text. There is no way to avoid them altogether. However, there are cases where you will need to eliminate hyphens. A bad hyphenation is when you break a word in a way that is awkward and confusing. For example:

- Contractions – never hyphenate contractions. It will break before the "n't" portion of the word and you do not want that starting the next line.

- Proper names – this one is not a hard-fast rule, just a suggestion. If possible try not to hyphenate a proper name, such as the name of a key figure or place, particularly the first time it appears.

- Compound words – If you have two words joined by a hyphen to create a compound word, do not introduce a second hyphen into the word or allow the automatic hyphenation to remain. Adjust the spacing until the line breaks on the existing hyphen or the compound word is all on one line.

- Breaking across pages – Hyphens can be disruptive at the best of times, even worse if two parts of the same word are on separate pages. If you can't adjust the hyphen out in the paragraph where it occurs, see if there is another paragraph where you can adjust the spacing to drop the last line to the next page so that the hyphenation is at least occuring on the same page. You can do this by adjusting the tracking (spacing between characters) or the leading (the spacing between lines.)

While not bad or wrong, you also want to avoid having too many lines ending in hyphens on the page. It just looks sloppy. A few will be unavoidable, but I generally try to have no more than three on a page, where possible. However, you won't always be able to adjust the spacing to eliminate a hyphen. Even when it is possible, you could find that eliminating the hyphen causes another problem. You have to decide which is the lesser of two evils, (or, if it is your own work, you could just revise the text to remove the issue.)

Lastly, while not technically wrong, I try to avoid hyphenation in the first or last line of a paragraph. You can't always, but it does feel more glaringly evident to me at those two points.

Hyphen- or Word-Stacking. Related to the above but a different issue, this is when you have more than one sentence in a row that either ends a hyphen or ends in the same word. This creates an uncomfortable visual pattern, and, in the case of the repeated word, can visually confuse the reader into losing their place.

Improper Alignment. The primary body of your text should always be justified (the text running from one side of the page to the other, with both sides aligning in a straight edge.) This creates a clean visual on the page that is easy to read and looks professional. While you may make the design choice to set portions of your text that are not justified (such as poems and letters) this should not be standard throughout.

Improper Spacing. This manifests in a variety of ways, but in general is when some spacing is visually excessive. For example:

- Double-spacing – Manuscript formatting is very different from publication formatting. While a manuscript should always be double-spaced to make it easier for an editor to read and allow them room to mark corrections, a printed book should never be double-spaced. The leading (or space between the printed lines) should be two points higher than the font size. (10 point font, gets a 12 point leading). Some publishers elect to make leading three points higher for a more comfortable read, depending on the font, due to irregularities in characters that extend above or below the line.

- Misaligned pages – This is when facing pages do not line up at the bottom of the page, ie, one page has more white space at the bottom. Text blocks should always be consistent in size when the pages face each other. This does not apply to facing pages where one is the end of a chapter and the other is the start of the next chapter.

- Excessive tracking – Remember on the previous page where I mentioned chosing the lesser of two evils? When you are adjusting your spacing to correct the other pitfalls listed in this section it is possible to over-correct, causing a more unsightly issue than the original problem. You may get rid of the hyphen or the bad break, but it causes too much or too little space between words or characters. You don't want one line to be very loosely spaced and the next one crammed together until you can hardly tell where one word ends and the other begins.

In some cases it is better to leave the original issue, with the understanding that you can't fix everything. An extra hyphen (in most cases) is less obtrusive than irregular text spacing. Always use the minimum of adjustment possible to correct an issue. When a reader looks at your book, it should be a seamless experience.

Improperly Placed Running Heads. Most pages in your book will include a running head, but there are instances where you would omit this, such as the opening page of a section, chapter, or story, and blank pages. This is where your templates come in. Most design programs have a way for you to create a template for each unique type of page you might use. You can also manually delete or change elements as needed.

Inconsistent Formatting. When you set a style for an element in your book, such as how the title will appear, or if the first paragraph of a page starts with a drop cap, it is important to be consistent and implement that formatting throughout your work. Most design programs and even word processing programs include tools that allow you to set style sheets or style guides to make it easier to format consistently. In most cases, it is just a matter of selecting the text element you wish to format and clicking on the style you have established. And the best thing, if you set a style sheet, if you need to change the formatting you can change the style sheet and it will update all instances where that style sheet was used so they all remain consistent.

Widows and Orphans. Most of us have heard of this taboo. How many of us actually know what it means? I am embarrassed to say that until last year my understanding was flawed. I can remember always being told to avoid them, but can't recall anyone explaining the issue in detail. For those who don't know, a widow is when the first line of a paragraph appears on one page and the rest of the paragraph is on the next page. And an orphan is when the last line of a paragraph falls on the next page.

It doesn't matter if it is one word or a full line, you want to avoid this.

For widows or short orphans, adjust the leading in the preceding paragraphs slightly so that one line moves to the next page, dealing with the orphan. To deal with longer orphans, you can adjust the tracking in the paragraph to add a little extra space on select lines to bump a word to the next line until there are two lines on the next page, instead of just one.

Summing Up

Don't get me wrong...this is by no means a comprehensive list of the potential pitfalls out there in the book-design world. I could likely write you an entire book on the fiddly bit things that can go wrong when typesetting—before you say it, I know, we don't actually *typeset* anymore, but since when has that ever stopped an industry from maintaining the lingo?—in any case, I have covered the most common issues encountered.

The key is to be consistent, clean, and professional. If you are adding space, don't add so much it is obvious what you have done. If you have set a style, don't change that style halfway through the book and make sure you use the correct style every time that design element appears.

Basically, check and double check that your book remains true to the blueprint from start to finish, and address unforeseen issues if and when they come up. If you do a proper job of it, the reader will never know there were issues along the way.

Chapter 7
Standard Amenities

Front Matter

There are two types of front matter, the kind that should appear in every book as a part the standard construction (Title, Copyright, and Contents* pages), and those the author chooses to include (Review Blurbs, Other Titles List, Dedication, Acknowledgements, and supplementary materials). The order these appear is pretty standard:

Review Blurbs. If a book has a number of high-profile positive reviews from sources that carry weight in the genre or industry, a page can be added before the title page where these can be included to entice potential readers. This page does not include a running head or page number.

Half-Title Page. A relic from another era, still used by printers who produce their books by offset or sheet-fed presses to prevent too many blank pages at the back of the book. Occasionally used by POD publishers when they have information they want to appear on a page facing the title page. This page does not include a running head or page number. If there is a Review Blurbs page a Half-Title Page would not be needed.

Other Titles List. Typically, this is on a left-hand page facing the title page. It includes other books by the author or anthologies or collections including the author's work. If the book is published through a publishing house, this list tends to include just books by

---
*Only in books where sections are distinctly identified with titles and/or authors.

that publisher. This page does not include a running head or page number.

Title Page. This is generally the first page in the book, but not always. The exceptions are listed above. They are optional and not always used. There will always be a title page and it will always be a right-hand page. There is no page number or running head. All a title page does is list the title, author, and publisher/imprint, and perhaps the series name, if there is one.

Regarding layout and design, one practice is to match the text treatment from the front cover, only in black and white. This can be done easily by extracting the text layer from the cover file in your art program and saving it as a separate file in black and white or grayscale, (depending on the available settings) then importing the title page as an image file. You can also replicated it in your desktop publishing software by retyping the text using the same fonts and styles so that it is an approximation of the cover text without matching it exactly.

Copyright Page. This should be the page directly following the title page, so it prints on the back of it. It should always be a left-hand page and there is no running head or page number. It includes the publisher's contact information, copyright notice, ISBN, Library of Congress Control Number (LCCC), any legal disclaimers, and production/art credits. Occasionally, publishers might include additional information here, such as if a series has a dedicated website, or if the author is available for events. It all depends on the space available.

If the book or part of the book has been published previously elsewhere that information will also be included on the copyright page, though I have seen it also placed on a separate acknowledgements page. Placement is at the publisher's discretion, as long as the information is included. This is a courtesy to the previous publisher, but also a courtesy to the reader so they don't pick up the book thinking it is new content, when they might have read all or part of it before.

Dedication. This is optional, but nice. Most books have one. The dedication can appear on the top of the copyright page, if there is room, or on a separate right-hand page facing the copyright page. If on a separate page, there is no page number or running head. A book can be dedicated to a loved one, in memory of someone lost, to someone you look up to, your hero...whatever you want. I once dedicated a book to "Albatrosses Everywhere" which seemed apropos for a collection titled *Consigned to the Sea*. A dedication should be either of special relevance to you as the author, or of some significance to the theme of the book.

Acknowledgements. This would start on a right-hand page. If it is one page long, there is no running head or page number, if it is longer than one page the subsequent pages do have running heads and page numbers.

Sometimes, an author wants to recognize family, friends, or professionals whose efforts were particularly noteworthy in making the book happen. Those that cheered them on, those who helped polish the manuscript, those who gave the author a chance to achieve their goal, or just someone who inspired them. This is what the Acknowledgements page is for. It is where the author thanks those who played some part in the realization of the dream.

However, it can also be where the publisher/author acknowledges previous publications of the work, particularly if, as in the case of a collection, there are multiple listings and insufficient room to include the information on the copyright page.

Contents Page (or Table of Contents). If the work is a novel and the author has only numbered the chapters and not titled them, there is no need for a contents page, unless the author includes additional content that is noteworthy, such as appendixes, excerpts, bonus stories, or glossaries. In that case, the author may chose to use a contents page so the reader is aware of the other content. With an anthology, collection, or nonfiction book a contents page is used to denote where stories, chapters, or other types of content appear in the book. This should start on a right-hand page. If it is one page long, there is no running head or page number, if it is longer than one page the subsequent pages do have running heads and page numbers.

Introduction. This is a part of the front matter, but would appear after the contents page (if there is one,) and would be included on it, whereas most of the other front matter elements would appear before the contents page and would not be cited. This would start on a right-hand page. If it is one page long, there is no running head or page number, if it is longer than one page the subsequent pages do have running heads and page numbers.

Introductions appear at the front of collections, anthologies, or textbooks and can be written by the editor, a respected professional in a related industry, or by a celebrity of some sort relevant to the content of the book. They could be written by the author themselves, but more often it is an endorsement by someone whose name carries weight. If the author writes it, it is more typically called a Foreword, A Note From the Author, Author's Note, or some other variation.

Supplementary Materials. Primarily with fiction or historic nonfiction, authors may chose to include bonus information at the beginning of the book to assist the reader in keeping details straight. Things like maps, timelines, lists of characters, and pronunciation guides for names and made-up or foreign words. Depending on what the material is and what space is available would determine where this information goes. Maps can go anywhere, but typically are before the title page, or right before the book proper begins. Lists and pronunciation guides appear after the dedication or Acknowledgements. If they are extensive, such information would more likely be included in the back matter, but it really depends on personal choice. This is the type of material that is non-standard to begin with, so there aren't really any rules. It is important to note, though, that if there is too much supplementary material at the beginning of your book, many readers have a habit of skipping it to get to the story.

Maps would have no running head or page number. Other types of supplementary material would start on a right-hand page. If they are one page long, there is no running head or page number, if they are longer than one pag,e the subsequent pages do have running heads and page numbers.

Back Matter

The following are the types of content that appear in the back of books. I have tried to put them roughly in the order I would expect them to appear, but to be truthful, I don't know that there are any hard and fast rules for what order things appear in the back matter.

Afterword. Similar to the Foreword, only it comes at the end of the book. It is where you as the author have a chance to expound on aspects of the book that you wouldn't want to talk about in the beginning before the reader is familiar with the content, either because the reader wouldn't get the references, or because you don't want to start off with spoilers. In the afterword, you can give a bit of insight into what inspired you, how the book came to be, or the challenges you faced in writing it.

Appendixes. Sometimes when you are researching or world-building for a novel you end up with more detail than you can feasibly include in the story without disrupting the flow or slowing down the pacing. This is content that can be included as Appendixes in the back of the book. If there are several different types of content, each one would be a separate Appendix. For example, if you have a scientific theory you researched and then extrapolated from, that would be one Appendix, but a detailed back story lending to the history of the universe would be a separate Appendix. Bonus content is nice, but don't overdo it. The more extra content you have, the longer the book. The longer the book, the more it costs to produce. The more it costs, the harder it might be to sell.

Glossary. If your book includes details or terms your reader may not be familiar with, you might want to include a glossary at the back of the book that provides expanded detail on those items so you aren't bogging your writing down with excessive explanation and the reader has a source to check if they get the details confused or want to know more if they are not familiar with a reference. These are alphabetical definition-style entries, with pronunciation guides (where applicable), definitions and origins of words or terms, and brief biographical entries on key characters. With a glossary, you have the option of going into greater detail than might be appropriate in the book itself.

Index. More applicable to nonfiction books, an index is where you list key terms and people mentioned in the book and what page numbers they appear on so that a reader can quickly locate specific information. Many programs have features that allow you to build indexes as you go along, but be wary of building your index in a word processing program. Often features like this do not import properly into a layout and design program because the coding is different. If your book has an index, this would be the last thing in the book, excepting, perhaps, your bio, depending on where you decide to place it.

Excerpts. With fiction books, it is not uncommon for a publisher (or author) to include excerpts from other works in the back of the book. This accomplishes two things: one, it lets the reader know there is more content out there; two, if the book is a little short an excerpt can help flesh it out to a desired page count. Sometimes they are excerpts of other books in the series, or just other books the author has written. Keep it short, and if it is not a related book, keep it relevant. (i.e. Don't put a hardcore science fiction excerpt in the back of an urban fantasy.) There isn't exactly a rule against it, but the audience for one genre doesn't always overlap with the audience of a different genre. Since excerpts are meant to entice readers to want to read the next thing, best to keep the content similar.

Bibliography/Sources. If you did any amount of research for your book, whether it is fiction or nonfiction, it is a good idea to include a listing of the sources you used in the back of the book, both to show you have factual contexts, and so that the reader can go to those sources for additional information, if they like. Of course, if you are writing nonfiction, you also want to cite your sources so you can't be accused of plagiarism.

About the Author. You put in a lot of work to write, format, and publish that book. Don't forget to tell them who you are and what else you've done. Some authors include personal details, others stick to their professional creds. Others interject humor and tailor their biography to the project at hand. However you approach it, things your bio should always contain are your name (duh), your publishing credits, and any major awards you may have received. Placement of this page varies. Some publishers put it right after the end of the book, and others put it after any back matter, so it is the last thing in the book. I have even seen publishers that put it in the front of the book…though I wouldn't recommend it.

In the case of anthologies, author bios can be handled in one of two ways. First, you could run the bio at the end of the author's story or chapter. Second, you could have a section at the back of the book where all the author bios run back to back either alphabetically or in the order they appear in the book.

Often, bios are also included for the editor or editors, and the artists, where applicable, those would always be at the back of the book.

Summing up

I am sure there are other types of front and back matter I haven't touched on here that are project-specific. There will always be variations, and for those you will have to use your judgment on what would look the most professional and best enhance the reader's experience.

As this book isn't about the technical aspects of writing, I will just say here that there are resources such as the Internet and style guides that can show you the proper way to write an index, glossary entry, or bibliographic reference. Seek those sources out and figure out which one suits your needs. Or, if you are doing design work freelance, confirm with your client if there is a particular style guide you should be following.

Just keep in mind, if you establish a style for something and that instance comes up again, whether in the same book or in a future project, remaining consistent to that style is an important part of establishing professionalism and building credibility. Sometimes, in this industry, that is all you have.

Text Checklist

Front Matter

- Does the title page include the title, author, and imprint or icon representing your company or brand?
- Does the copyright page include your company/brand and contact information, copyright information, standard disclaimer, and art credits?
- Do you have a dedication or acknowledgements page?
- If applicable, do you have a Contents page and do the chapter/story titles/author names match what is listed on the corresponding pages in the book? Are the page numbers correct?

Chapter/Story Opening Page

- Is the running head removed from this page?
- Is there comfortable space at the top of the page, with the title or chapter offset from the text copy?

Running Head/Foot

- Is the page number clear and visible, either at the outer edge of the running head, or centered or on the outer edge in the running foot?
- Is the title and author name clear, legible, but not overwhelming in the running head?

- Is there a comfortable space between the running head and the text block?

Text Block

- Is your font clear and readable?
- Is your text block justified (from margin to margin)?
- Is the spacing between lines comfortable? Not too open or too dense?
- Have you corrected for widows and orphans (one line of a paragraph alone at the top or bottom of a page)?
- Have you avoided having multiple lines ending with a hyphen or the same word stacked together?
- Have you adjusted the spacing to avoid hyphenated contractions or double-hyphenated words?
- Do you have a section break that complements your text without overwhelming it?

Illustrations/Graphic Treatment

- Does your graphic treatment complement the theme of your story?
- Are your illustrations properly placed in relation to the text they are related to?
- If applicable, do your illustrations have a corresponding citation that is noted in the relevant text?
- Are the images clean and clear? Are the lines crisp and solid? Do they complement the text?
- Is the art/image style consistent throughout the book?

Back Matter

- Did you include an up-to-date author biography?

- Have you included an excerpt? Is it genre-appropriate to your book?
- Do you have a glossary, if so have you included all the unique terms/primary characters in your book? Is it properly alphabetized?
- Does your book have an index? Is it properly formatted and does it include all relevant terms and key references?
- Does your book have references? Are they properly/consistently formatted and complete?

Part Three - Bonus Content

Chapter 8
But Wait, There's More...

What? You didn't think that was everything, did you? I covered the basics, things you encounter in any book, for the most part. Publishing, however, is rarely that simple. There are niche markets and specialty publishing and all kinds of books with rules of their own (how else can we break them, right?).

Consider this a bonus chapter touching on some of the most common specialty books with unique formatting to consider.

Epistolary Novels. Have you ever read a book that is nothing but a series of letters or journal entries, with little to no narrative in between? That is an epistolary novel. In most ways they are very much like any other book. They may be segmented into chapters, or they may just run from letter to letter until the end. I don't know that there is a set form since it is not a frequently used format.

The key is consistency. Create set formats for the specific elements and carry those through in every instance. For example, if this is a modern interpretation of an epistolary novel it could be told in an email format:

> FROM: joe@mail.com   March 31, 2020, 4:44pm
> TO: you@email.com
> SUBJECT: The Message I Wrote
>
> Do tell.
>
> On Mar 30, 2020, at 8:45 PM, You Yourself <you@email.com> wrote:
>
>> >This is all I have to say.

This goes for letters, texts, memos, or any other type of correspondence (collectively called missives) through which a tale could be told. Use the format conventions associated with that style of communication, but don't go too crazy or it could be difficult to carry out through a full book or for a reader to even read. A simplistic but recognizable representation on the page will more deeply immerse the reader in the story.

If you are intermixing narrative between the letters, format things in such a way that there is a clear distinction between the different elements. Generally, this is done by making the missives italics, but I would not recommend that if most or all of the book is epistolary. It can be taxing on the readers' eyes. Another way to address this is to have the narrative in a conventional font, and the missives in a distinctly different font.

Whatever style you set, always keep in mind it should be consistent, clean, and easy to read.

Poetry Books. The major difference between a book of poetry and a book of prose is in the text block. Pretty much all the other elements are consistent. Here is a list of elements specific to poetry:

- A new poem starts a new page, unless they are very short, such as a haiku, and you chose to put several on one page. If this is the case, make sure it is clear they are separate poems. You should not, however, have a short poem followed by a long poem that runs to another page. It is acceptable to have a short poem follow a long poem, if there is sufficient space for it to appear fully on the page.

- If a poem does not have a title you generally put (untitled) at the top so it is clear it is the start of a new poem and that would be formatted in the style of the title formatting.

- The first page of a poem is generally handled the same as a chapter opening page, with distinctive styles for the title and poet, if applicable, and a simple style for the poem itself.

- If the collection consists of poems all by one poet, the poet's name would appear on the cover, the title page, and in the running head, but not on each poem.

- It is a design choice of how you will handle the running head. I have seen poetry books where the first page of the poem (as with chapters or stories) does not have a running head, but subsequent pages do have one. This is tricky, though, especially if most but not all of the poems are just one page long. Because of this dilemma, some designers put a running head at the top of every page in a poetry book and titles are treated in a simple manner. It is really up to you. As long as you are consistent in your choices and take into account the overall visual esthetic as it applies to your particular book, either choice is acceptable from an industry standard.

- Page numbers are generally centered at the bottom of the page in the running foot, especially if there is no running head or the running head only appears on certain pages.

- Alignment is either flush left, flush right, or centered, not justified. Unless there is a special case where lines or stanzas are specifically arranged as a visual part of the experience, alignment and indent should be consistent from poem to poem.

- While the page has standard margins, poems are generally indented so they are closer to the center of the page even if they are not center-aligned.

- Watch your spacing. If you need to run a poem to the next page and it has short stanzas, break it in between stanzas, not in the middle of them.

- With the exception of the first poetry page of the book, poems can start on a left or right page. Unless the book is divided into sections, there is no need to have a blank page in a volume of poetry.

Cookbooks. Again, as with most of these niche formats, all the basics still apply. A cookbook would have both a contents page and an index. It could potentially have Appendixes depending on the level of detail you want to provide.

Here is where things are different:

- The recipe name serves as the title.
- Ingredients list showing amounts and units of measure in a consistent format throughout, plus any specific preparation instructions (i.e. 1 cup of carrots, diced). This can be the total of each ingredient needed, or you can break it out for how much of the ingredients are needed for each stage of the recipe, in the order they are used. With this method, just as an example, the ingredients list for a dutch apple pie recipe would have butter listed two times, two tablespoons to dot the pie filling, and one stick to make the crumb top.
- Materials list showing what tools will be needed, per the instructions. Not every cookbook does this, but I find it helpful so I always include one.
- How many servings the recipe makes.
- Temperature to pre-heat to if the recipe is oven-based.
- Detailed instructions in the order they need to be executed.
- Helpful hints or recommendations.
- Variations or substitutions.

Cookbooks can be simplistic and text-based, or they can be full-color with photographs and side bars and all the bells and whistles. When you are ready to make your design choices take a field trip to your local bookstore and check out the cookbook section. That is the best way to get a feel for the design choices you can make.

Game Manuals. Now here is where things get interesting…and confusing. This type of book is what I would call a chimera. It is almost always part technical manual and part art book, with production values dependent on available resources and budget (not always the same thing.) It is difficult to tell you what to include where because layout and creative design are so tightly woven together in this format.

Here are the basics of what you usually find:

- Overview/Introduction to Game Mechanics
- The Game Universe
- Character Types
- Basic Skill Sets
- Advanced Skill Sets
- Weaponry
- Equipment/Techology/Magic/ Spells/etc.
- Non-Player Characters/Opponents/Monsters/Aliens/etc.
- Combat Mechanics
- Game Scenarios
- Quick Reference Charts

While there is typically a stylistic design running throughout the book, there may be a number of variations on page templates depending on the information being conveyed. Creating style sheets or templates for each different type of page you need streamlines the process. They can always be adjusted for special situations. As for formatting, much of it is design choice, but here are some standard design elements you should know:

Trim Size. Most game manuals take their format from a technical manual. As much data as possible is put on one page to facilitate ease of use and access to information during game play. With this in mind, the trim size of these books usually falls between 8 x 10 or 8.5 x 11, depending on the method of print and available paper sizes.

Icons/Tabs. Pretty much every game manual I have ever seen has had the different sections of the book identified by an icon or a tab on the outer edge of the page, either in the same place at the top of the page or along the outside edge of the page with each section being at a different point on the edge so that players or game masters can easily find the information they need. Kind of the way some dictionaries have cut-outs so you can find the section for each letter easily.

Text Block. Text more often than not flows in two or three columns to a page, with first line indented and justified text. This is, of course, modified if part of the page is taken up by data blocks.

Sidebars. This is related information that is not included in the main text, but is broken out in a side section. For example, if you have a three-column text block on the page but want to reference other information that is relevant without getting confusing you might have the standard text block only run two columns instead of three, and in the space that would have been the third column there is a separate information block with this collateral information. Often it is set off in some way, with a colored or shaded background, or maybe in a box, so that it is clear this is side information and not a continuation of the standard text.

Data blocks. Whether it is text or diagrams, tables or charts, game manuals deal in data. Relevant data should be grouped together in a logical manner in sections and cross-referenced as needed when the data is applied in the manual. If the data element is complicated, with many columns, it is a good idea to differentiate entries by either alternately highlighting every other entry, or dividing entries with a line between each one to make for easier tracking across the columns.

Graphics, Tables, and Charts. These should be well marked and easy to read, with the same style used throughout the book for uniformity and clarity.

The key to game manuals is consistency in how you convey the information. Often there will be a comprehensive table or chart laying out the game mechanics as it applies to different things, such as combat, damage, etc. Then later as elements of those charts apply to specific character types or situations, the relevant data is extracted from the comprehensive chart and replicated in a case-specific version of that chart, using the same formatting but in a smaller scale.

Summing Up

I know. There is someone out there wondering why I didn't cover x, y, or z. There are two camps on the matter. 1) everything else is just variations on what I have covered here; or 2) everything else is so stylistic that there are no "basics" to focus on.

With that in mind, if I missed something you were hoping I would cover, you can contact me and I might have some details I could share. If not, your best bet — as I have mentioned — is to go to where those books are and take a look at some examples in the wild. If one book did it, but the others didn't, it is likely a design choice. If you see elements that many of them used, that make it closer to a standard design element.

As always, in the end, your mantra should be clean, clear, and consistent.

Afterword

I know. I know. It's a lot to take in. Take a moment. Breathe.

If I've done my job right, you now have the blueprint to build better books. A starting place to improve your craft.

Yes. I said starting place. It is an ongoing process.

Book design and layout takes effort and practice. It isn't easy to keep all the fine details straight and to make sure everything is in its place. Often, even when you do everything exactly as you should, things go wrong. It might be because you didn't realize you activated a particular setting or you clicked on something you shouldn't have with the wrong tool selected. It might be because the program glitched and isn't doing what it is supposed to the way it is supposed to. Or it might be because you imported hidden code from your word-processing program without realizing it.

I once typeset a book five times from scratch because of such a hidden code.

To say I wasn't happy about it is a gross understatement, particularly when I discovered why things had glitched. But trust me, each time you work on a book you will learn something new. Every time you venture into the program you are going to use you will discover a new trick or a new tool that will make the next project easier. Don't be afraid to try new things. Don't hesitate to explore the program and see what it can do and how it does it. And don't forget, every program has a help feature. Can't figure out what went wrong or how to do what you want to do? Look it up and see what answers are out there. Or seek out an online forum where others might have wisdom to share. Heck… head over to YouTube because you know there's a video for *everything* these days.

But most of all, don't give up. Enjoy yourself. Try new things. Be creative. Make magic!

There can never be too many books.

Appendix
Avoiding Some Mistakes I've Made

I know. I said this book wasn't about how to use the design programs. And I meant it, really. But that doesn't mean I can't share with you some simple tips on avoiding headaches I've encountered on my own path of learning.

Design Problem – My chapters have run all together instead of starting on a new page.

Preemptive Solution – In your word processing program, be sure to use Insert Page Break when a chapter ends to start the next chapter. This is an example of coding that does play well with the design program.

Design Problem – The words are oddly spaced in some of my sentences.

Preemptive Solution – There are two potential causes of this. The first one is that there might be manual line breaks in the manuscript. Before you import your text into your design program make sure to "Find and Replace" all manual line breaks (in Microsoft Word the coding for this is ^|), replacing them with a (space) or a paragraph mark (^p) as appropriate.

The other cause is when you have words or phrases linked by a / or ... so that the program interprets the whole grouping as one word. The way to fix this is to insert a hair space or thin space before or after the slash or ellipsis. These are small enough they aren't visible, but are enough to break the grouping so the program doesn't see it as one word. Search in your design program for Add Character (In QuarkXpress this is under the Utilities Menu.)

Design Problem – My footnotes/endnotes have integrated with my text.

Preemptive Solution – Do not use the formatting tools in your word processing program to create footnotes in your manuscript before you import it into your design program. Either designate them manually, or create the footnotes/endnotes using the tools in the design program after you import the text.

If you try to do it in the word processing program the note will be linked to the text where it is relevant and it will end up integrated within the text instead of appearing at the bottom of the page or at the back of the book.

Design Problem – The text is leaving large gaps at the bottom of the page.

Preemptive Solution – Before you import your text into your design program make sure to turn off the widow and orphan control and the settings that force lines to remain together. If that doesn't work, you will need to save your source file as a text only document to strip it of existing code and then reformat things like italic or special characters in the new file.

Design Problem - | # | - this code…don't know what it is or what it does, but I used this combination of symbols (with the # representing an actual number) as a decorative section break and when I tried to generate a PDF of the text it failed every time. I discovered the culprit when I tried creating a PDF of the book chapter by chapter and the chapter containing this treatment continued to fail.

Preemptive Solution – Don't do that. And more constructively, see if your design program has a feature that lets you see hidden code.

Design Problem – When I import text it is all in the wrong format.

Preemptive Solution – Before you import text, in the design program click on the *No Style* option in your standard style sheets, then import your text. It should retain all of the original formatting.

Design Problem – When I try to export Text from the design program, parts of it are missing.

Preemptive Solution – Do not import your text elements into your design program piecemeal. Create one manuscript file for your project before importing it. That way all the text blocks are linked together. Otherwise, you will have to identify each separate text block and export the text individually, then combine them into one file in your word processing program.

Design Problem – When I generate the PDF for print my blank pages disappear.

Preemptive Solution – In your design program, before you create your PDF, click on the Options button in the window that pops up when you select Export as PDF. In the window that opens when you click Options click the check box that says 'Include Blank Pages'.

Design Problem – When I upload my production files to the printer I get the error message that my text uses Spot Colors.

Preemptive Solution – With a black-and-white book, it is important that your text be in solid black. Sometimes black text in your word processing program comes across as a spot color when imported into the design program. After you import your text, select all text and then go to the color selector and designate the text to be just 'Black'.

Design Problem – When I upload my production files to the printer I get the error message that my file includes layers.

Preemptive Solution – Before you create your PDF, click on the Options button in the window that pops up when you select Export as PDF. In the window that opens when you click Options, click on the Layers option, once on that tab make sure the box that says 'Create PDF Layers' is not checked.

Design Problem – Have more questions?

Preemptive Solution – Drop me an email at especbooks@aol.com with *Build-A-Book Question* in the subject line.

About the Author

Award-winning author and editor **Danielle Ackley-McPhail** has worked both sides of the publishing industry for longer than she cares to admit. In 2014, she joined forces with husband Mike McPhail and friend Greg Schauer to form her own publishing house, eSpec Books (www.especbooks.com).

Her published works include six novels, *Yesterday's Dreams, Tomorrow's Memories, Today's Promise, The Halfling's Court, The Redcaps' Queen,* and *Baba Ali and the Clockwork Djinn,* written with Day Al-Mohamed. She is also the author of the solo collections *Eternal Wanderings, A Legacy of Stars, Consigned to the Sea, Flash in the Can, Transcendence, Between Darkness and Light,* and the nonfiction writers' guides, *The Literary Handyman* and *LH: Build-A-Book Workshop.*

She is the senior editor of the award-winning *Bad-Ass Faeries* anthology series, *Gaslight & Grimm, Side of Good/Side of Evil, After Punk,* and *Footprints in the Stars.* Her short stories are included in numerous other anthologies and collections.

In addition to her literary acclaim, she crafts and sells original costume horns under the moniker The Hornie Lady Custom Costume Horns, and homemade flavor-infused candied ginger under the brand of Ginger KICK! at literary conventions, on commission, and wholesale.

Danielle lives in New Jersey with husband and fellow writer, Mike McPhail and three extremely spoiled cats.

To learn more about her work, visit www.sidhenadaire.com or www.especbooks.

Acknowledgements – This generally goes at the front of the book, though some publishers choose to put it at the back. It is a list or written section where you acknowledge those who helped make the book possible, helped work on it, or supported you while you wrote it.

Appendixes – This is additional or expanded information presented at the end of the book. It is a way for the author to share research, theories, or back story without interrupting the flow of the story or text when the additional information might not be immediately relevant, just of interest.

Back Matter – The extra content located at the back of your book, such as but not limited to the author's biography, Appendixes, Glossary, or Index. Content that is separate from your story or nonfiction, but complements it.

Bar Code – A graphic representation of the ISBN (see below). It is made up of bars of varying widths that represent the individual numbers that make up the ISBN. It is traditionally printed on the back cover.

Bleed – This is extra space that you add to your cover design where the image or background color extends past the boundary of your final trim size. The bleed is there to provide a safety zone when the cover is trimmed down to size by the printer. This ensures that you do not end up with a white border along the edge of your cover if the trim is a little off.

Blurb – The text that appears on the back cover (or jacket flaps, in the case of a hardcover) that describes the book, enticing the reader to want to know more. Also called Cover Copy, Cover Blurb, Book Blurb, or Jacket Copy.

Chapter/Story Title – The identifying text that appears on the first page of your chapter, story, or article, depending on if you are producing a novel, collection/anthology, or nonfiction work.

CMYK – This is a color profile, or mode, that stands for Cyan, Magenta, Yellow, and Black. That means that every color on your cover is made up of different values of some combination of those four colors.

Contents Page – Also called the Table of Contents. The list of sections that appear in your book, including titles and page numbers. If the book involves contributions by multiple individuals, the author's name would appear following the title of their work. This only includes materials that come after the contents page.

Copyright Page – The page following the title page, including the relevant details and disclaimers required in publishing, such as, but not limited to, the publisher's contact information, the copyright notice, the relevant ISBNs, Library of Congress Control Number, and legal disclaimers, also included are the credits for the cover art, any illustrations, the editor, and the designer(s).

Cover Template – A file provided by the printer showing the exact dimension of your book cover, including guidelines indicating where the cover will be folded and trimmed. Templates also include your basic book data, the bar code matching your ISBN, and markings indicating the minimum safe zones for where you can place your text and important elements of your artwork. Templates are provided electronically as PDFs or InDesign files.

DPI – Stands for Dots Per Inch. The clarity of all images is measured in DPI. The more dots per inch, the clearer an image is. The less dots per inch, the more jaggy an image is. The higher the DPI, the bigger the file will be.

Drop Cap – When the first letter of the first word on a page is larger and inset into the first paragraph by two or more lines. Often the font is different and more ornate than that used for the base text. Take care which font you choose as some have florishes that will obsure the surrounding text. The font should be easy to read and complement the feel of the book.

Facing Pages – These are pages that will be visible side by side when you open the book. In other words, you can see them at the same time without turning the page. You can think of it this way, if you close the book they are facing each other. Well…more than facing, but what happens behind closed covers…

Folio – The technical term for the page number.

Front Matter – The extra content located at the front of a book, such as but not limited to the title page, Table of Contents, dedication, maps, list of characters, list of terms, or pronunciation guides. This material is generally numbered with lowercase roman numerals when there is a page number on the page. A running head or page number is generally only used if the element (such as the contents page) is longer than one page.

Full-Bleed – When a background or image extends all the way to the edge of the printed page. To allow for this and make sure there is no white space where there shouldn't be, the designer extends the background or image a quarter inch past the desired trim size of the book.

Glossary – A list of terms that generally appears in the back matter giving greater detail regarding terms or concepts depicted in the book.

Gutter Margin – The extra space you should add to your text design on the inside edge of the page where the book will eventually be bound. Typically, you would add a quarter of an inch or more depending on the thickness of the book. This extra space allows the book to be bound without the text disappearing into the binding of the book.

Half-Title Page – The same as the title page, but with only the title of the book printed on it, not the author and the publisher. When there is a half-title page, it is generally the first page in the book, followed by a blank page, a list of other titles by the author, or a quote or image the author wishes to start off the book with. Half-title pages are a legacy from offset or sheet-fed printing, where a book's pagination must be in increments of four-, eight-, or sixteen-page signatures. If there are too many blank pages at the end of the book (which looks bad) a half-title page is included in the front matter to adjust the signatures and reduce the number of blank pages in the back. In digital printing a half-title page might be included if there is some design element the author or publisher wants to include on the page facing the title page.

Imprint – The brand under which the book is being produced. Sometimes this is the publisher's name, but sometimes a publisher will create a separate sub-brand to group books by genre or type.

Index – These are used for nonfiction, textbooks, and cookbooks. It is a list of the relevant terms in the book and where they are discussed so that readers can go directly to the passages that may contain the information they are looking for.

Introduction – Some books will have an introduction. In most cases, these are collections or nonfiction books. The introduction may be written by the author, or by a notable individual, such as a professional in the industry or a well-known author.

ISBN – International Standard Book Number. A unique identifier assigned by the publisher. Each version of a book requires its own ISBN, which is tied to basic data about the book, such as but not limited to publisher, title, author, format, page count, and price. The ISBN is used by booksellers and librarians to order your book and manage their inventory. All ISBNs are purchased via a service called Bowker. If you purchase from Bowker, the ISBN will show you as the publisher. ISBNs are expensive purchased individually through this service, but the price goes down when you buy in bulk. Standard options are one, ten, and one-hundred ISBNs, with the cost per number going down the more you order at once. If you obtain an ISBN through a publishing service, such as Kindle Direct or Ingram Spark, they are less expensive, or even free, but those numbers indicate that the company you received them from is the publisher of that book, which will also imply to those in the industry that it is self-published, whether it is or not.

Layout – 1. How the elements of your book are arranged on the page. 2. The act of arranging the elements of your book, including placement and style.

Logo – A graphic element representing your brand or imprint. The icon or design should be unique to you. Keep it simple so that it can be scaled up or down as needed and still be legible. It should also be distinct so that it can be readily identified as representing your company. You will want both a black-and-white version, for use in the interior, and a color version, for use on the cover. You will also want to use this logo for advertising purposes.

Margins – The blank space running around the edge of the text block denoting the edge of the page.

POD – Print on Demand. This is a digital printing method that allows you to print as few or as many copies as you need. Rather than a printing press, this method makes use of a more advanced copier-type printer where a book prints on standard paper sheets, which are trimmed down to the desired size.

Price-Specific Bar Code – A graphic representation of the ISBN. It is made up of bars of varying widths that represent the individual numbers that make up the ISBN. It also includes additional bars that represent the retail price you have set. You can find free software online that will generate any type of bar code you need. Your printer should also be provided one by your printer if you request a cover template file. There is no need to purchase a bar code, it is an unnecessary expense.

Review Blurbs – Occasionally, a book will include advance reviews or reviews of a previous edition. When these are particularly favorable and from a reputable source, publishers will often include these at the beginning of the book on the first page following the front cover.

RGB – A color profile, or mode, that stands for Red, Green, and Blue. That means that all the colors on your cover are made up of different values of some combination of these three colors.

Running Foot – When the page numbers appear consecutively at the bottom of the printed page.

Running Head – The text and/or page number that appears at the top of the printed page. For novels, it generally contains the title of the book on one page and the author's name on the facing page, both accompanied by the page number. For collections or anthologies, it generally contains the title of the book on one page with the story or article title and author on the facing page, both accompanied by the page number.

Section Break – A decorative element that appears between two separate sections of text, generally in a work of fiction. It can be a font-generated symbol or an actual art graphic that complements the theme of the book.

Sidebar - In textbooks, manuals, and cookbooks, these are text blocks that are separate from the main content, but convent additional information that is related or that the author feels might be useful, or highlights points they wish to emphasis.

Stock Art – Photographs, illustrations, or works of art that have been posted by an artist on a Stock Art website where individuals can purchase a non-exclusive license to use the art for use as interior illustrations or cover art. The cost of the license depends on which rights you wish to purchase and the cost will differ from site to site. There are subscriptions you can sign up for that reduce the overall cost. It is not unusual for artists to create portfolios on multiple sites and there is no limit to how many individuals may license that image. Once you secure the rights to use an image you are able to modify it or combine it with other art to suit your needs but must credit the original artist or artists on the copyright page of your book.

Style Guides – In many desktop publishing programs—if not all—there are tools where you can define the formatting for different aspects of your book so that when they reoccur all you need to do is select the correct style and the formatting will be implemented. The style guides also allow you to change the style of an element in one place and have it automatically apply to all instances of that style.

Templates – In many desktop publishing programs—if not all—you can create a standard template, or Master, for a type of page in your book that you can drop into place as needed changing the existing layout to the desired layout.

Text Treatment – The words that appear on your cover and any special effects you may employ to embellish them via an art program or internet site.

Title Page – This page includes the basic identifying information of a book. In most cases, the title, series, book number (where applicable), the author or editor's name, the imprint and the publisher's location.

Trim Size – The final dimensions of your printed book. A standard trim size for a Trade Paperback is six inches by nine inches (or 6 x 9). These dimensions are set, though the actual measurements of the book might vary slightly depending on how precisely the book is trimmed on the production line. The spine width of your book is determined by the weight of your paper and the number of pages in the finished book.

Construction Crew

A. L. Kaplan
A. Parsons
Allison E. Kaese
Alma Alexander
Anthony Stevens
Asahina Nakama
Barbara and Carl Kesner
Bradij
Carol Gyzander
Christopher Weuve
David Edelstein
David J. Schwartz
Frances Rowat
Frank & Lura Wilcox
Grig Larson
Jakub Narębski
Jaq Greenspon
Jenn Whitworth
Jim Gotaas
Joey Ruff
Johanna Rothman
Judi Fleming
Kathryn Scannell

KR
L.E. Custodio
Lindsay
Lorraine J. Anderson
Lucy A. Snyder
maileguy
Mary Fan
mdtommyd
Michael A. Burstein
Michael Mullen
Mike Fonseca
Mindie Jeanne Simmons
Nicholas Diak
Peter D Engebos
R.T. Bryson
Selene Tan
Sheryl R. Hayes
Spencer E. Hart
Tanith Korravai
The Rhatigans
Tina M Noe Good
Travis L Thomas
   (Humble Fox Books)

Index

#
10 point font 45
300 DPI 34, 50
3D modeling software 19
3D posing program 17
6 x 9 11, 46

A
About the Author 65
Acknowledgements 39, 59, 61
Adobe 3, 4, 18
Affinity 3
Afterword 63
alignment 44
Analog 30
anthologies 43, 47, 59, 61, 65
Appendixes 39, 61, 63
art 11, 14, 27, 51
art program 3, 14
artist credit 29
author 14
author bio 27
author name 43
awards 14, 27, 29, 65

B
back cover 27
back cover copy 29
back matter 39, 47, 63
bad breaks 46, 53
Bad cover art 17
bad cover designs 19
bad hyphenation 54
banner 27
bar code 9, 28, 33
bestseller 27, 29
bibliography 64
bleed 9, 33
book blurb 9
Bowker 4, 10
brand 10
bullet lists 49

C
Calibre 4
chapter opening page 43, 47, 50
Chapter/Story Title 39
charts 78
Chicago Manual of Style 49
citation 49
CMYK 9, 34
color profile 9, 11
composition 21
compound words 54
concept sketches 18
confusing art 20

contents page 39, 40, 61, 62
contractions 54
cookbooks 76
copyright 40, 51, 59
Copyright Page 39, 60
Corel Photopaint 3

correspondence 48
cover 7-35
cover art 3, 14, 29
cover blurb 9, 25, 27
Cover Copy 9
cover design 14-17, 31
cover design, iconic 14
cover design, iey elements 17
cover design, montage 17
cover design, stylistic 14
cover template 4, 10, 11, 32, 33
crop marks 33
Cyan, Magenta, Yellow, and Black 9

D
data blocks 78
Daz3d 3, 17
dedication 59, 60
design program 47
desktop publishing 4, 42
digital format 45
digital printing method 11
dots per inch 10
double-spacing 55
DPI 10, 34
drop cap 40, 44

E
ebook conversion program 4
embellishment 49
endnotes 49
epistolary novels 73
excerpts 61, 64
excessive tracking 56

F
facing pages 40, 44
family tree 51
file format 34
final dimensions 11, 33
final files 34
finalist 29
flashback 46
folio 40

font 45
footnotes 49
foreword 63
Fotolia 18
FoxIt 4
front matter 40, 59
full-bleed 40

G
game manuals 76
genre 29, 59
getting the details wrong 20
glossaries 39, 40, 61, 63
graphic embellishment 50
graphics 78
guidelines 34
Guttenberg 1
gutter margin 40, 46

H
half-title page 41, 59
header 53
how to pick art 14

I
icon 10, 23, 50, 78
illustrations 11, 50
imprint 10, 23, 28, 41
improper alignment 55
improper spacing 55
inconsistent formatting 56
indent 44, 45
independent publishing 19
index 41, 64
industry magazine 30
Ingram Spark 4
insert 53
International Standard
    Book Number 4, 10, 28
introduction 41, 62
ISBN 4, 10, 11, 28, 33, 40

J
jacket copy 9, 25
journal entries 73
JPEG 3, 34
justified 44, 54

K
kerning 46
kill fee 18
Kindle Direct Publishing 4

L
lack of contrast 20
layout 41
leading 45, 46, 55
legal disclaimers 40
letters 73
Library of Congress Control Number 40
license 50
line art 50
line spacing 46
lists of characters 62
logo 10, 41
lyrics 46, 48

M
manuscript format 45
maps 62
margins 41, 46
misaligned pages 56

N
negative space 21
Non-Distribution SKU 28
non-exclusive license 11
nonfiction 61
nonfiction books 50
Numbered Lists 49

O
offset printing 1, 41
Other Titles List 59

P
page humber 47
PDF 3, 4, 10, 33, 34
photographs 11, 19, 51
Photoshop 15
POD 11, 50, 59
poem 53
poetry 48
poetry books 74
point size 45, 47
portfolios 11
Poser 3, 17
predatory presses 1
price 29
price-specific bar code 11, 28, 29
print books 23
print format 45
Print on Demand 11
print-on-demand printing 24
production 33
professional review sites 30
pronunciation guides 62
proper names 54
Publishers Weekly 30
publishing 1
publishing credits 65

Q
QuarkXpress 4
quote 46, 48

R
readability 22, 23, 45
Red, Green, and Blue 11
review blurbs 14, 30, 42, 59
RGB 11, 34
rights 11
running foot 42
running head 42, 47, 56

S

sans serif font 45
section break 42, 48, 53
section title 53
series name 14
serif font 45
sheet-fed printing 1, 41
Shutterstock 18
sidebars 78
signatures 41
single-spaced 44
small press 14, 19, 53
sources 64
spacing 46
specialty publishing 73
spine 23
standard fonts 45
standard trim size 11
stanzas 75
stock art 11, 14, 18, 19, 50
Stock Keeping Unit 28
style guides 42, 47
subscription 11, 18
subsidy press 1
subtitle 14
superscript 49
supplementary materials 62

T

tables 46, 51, 78
teaser 25
templates 42, 47, 56
text block 37, 44, 47, 56, 78
text checklist 67
text treatment 11
textbook 43
the hook 25
TIFF 3, 34
timelines 51, 62
title 14
title page 42, 59, 60
trade paperback 11, 46
traditional publishers 28, 49, 53
trim size 11, 33, 77
typesetting 45, 53

U

unique identifier 10, 28

V

Vanity presses 1

W

website 29
white space 44, 53
widows and orphans 46, 57
winner 29
word-stacking 55

www.ingramcontent.com/pod-product-compliance
Lightning Source LLC
Chambersburg PA
CBHW020144130526
44591CB00030B/207